Test Your Chess Skills

Sarhan Guliev & Logman Guliev

Test Your Chess Skills

Practical Decisions in Critical Moments

New In Chess 2018

© 2018 New In Chess

Published by New In Chess, Alkmaar, The Netherlands
www.newinchess.com

Translated from the Russian book *Testi dlya kwalifitsirovannykh shakhmatistov*
by Sarhan Guliev & Logman Guliev (2018)

Cover design: Buro Blikgoed
Proofreading and supervision: Peter Boel
Translation: Steve Giddins
Editing and typesetting: Frank Erwich
Production: Anton Schermer

Have you found any errors in this book?
Please send your remarks to editors@newinchess.com. We will
collect all relevant corrections on the Errata page of our website
www.newinchess.com and implement them in a possible next edition.

ISBN: 978-90-5691-809-5

Contents

Explanation of symbols

The chessboard
with its coordinates:

±	White stands slightly better
∓	Black stands slightly better
±	White stands better
∓	Black stands better
+−	White has a decisive advantage
−+	Black has a decisive advantage
=	balanced position
!	good move
!!	excellent move
?	bad move
??	blunder
!?	interesting move
?!	dubious move

❑ White to move
■ Black to move
♔ King
♕ Queen
♖ Rook
♗ Bishop
♘ Knight

'Life is a game of chess.' – Miguel Cervantes

'We are in truth but pieces on this chess board of life, which in the end we leave, only to drop one by one into the grave of nothingness.' – Omar Khayyam

Authors' foreword

Anyone who began studying chess in the late 1970s or early 1980s will remember very well the remarkable book *The Best Move* by the two Czech Vlastimils – Hort and Jansa. The present authors are no exception. This unusual book, written in an original style (part puzzle book, part philosophical, somewhat satirical, but in all respects excellently done) remained forever in our memory. The years have passed and the 'former' readers (although we remain readers until the end of our days) and currently active players have themselves amassed many interesting games, filled with striking and instructive episodes. And sometimes they, as authors, want to share their finds with chess lovers. Thus was the present work born.

The authors have accompanied the examples with proverbs and quotations from well-known personalities, in a bid to underline the fact that chess and philosophy have much in common. We sincerely hope that in reading this book, you will again feel just what a wonderful game chess is, and will love it even more. New horizons of chess art will open up before you. The positions given are of varied character, and you will find striking tactical blows, deep strategic manoeuvres, opening traps, standard endgame devices, etc.

Good luck!

Sarhan & Logman Guliev
Baku, September 2018

Exercises

1
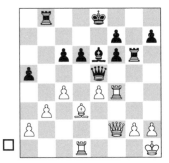

Is White's position:
  A) winning;
  B) better;
  C) equal?
(solution on page 65)

2

What would you play:
  A) 12...♘b6;
  B) 12...♕e7;
  C) 12...♘e8 ?
(solution on page 65)

3
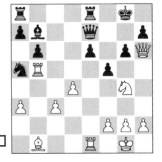

Is White's position:
  A) winning;
  B) hopeless;
  C) equal?
(solution on page 66)

4
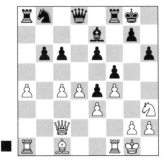

Is Black's position:
  A) better;
  B) worse;
  C) equal?
(solution on page 66)

5

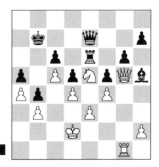

Is Black's position:
  A) better;
  B) worse;
  C) equal?

How should he play:
  A) 46...♔c7;
  B) 46...♕xg5 ?
(*solution on page 67*)

6

Is Black's position:
  A) winning;
  B) hopeless;
  C) equal?
(*solution on page 67*)

7

Is White's position:
  A) winning;
  B) hopeless;
  C) equal?
(*solution on page 68*)

8

Is White's position:
  A) better;
  B) worse;
  C) equal?
(*solution on page 68*)

9

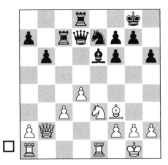

Is White's position:
  A) better;
  B) worse;
  C) equal?
(solution on page 69)

10

What would you play:
  A) 6...♘f6;
  B) 6...♘e7 ?
(solution on page 69)

11

Is White's position:
  A) better;
  B) worse;
  C) equal?
(solution on page 70)

12

Is Black's position:
  A) winning;
  B) hopeless;
  C) equal?
(solution on page 70)

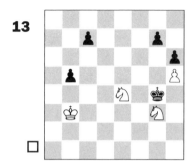

Is White's position:
A) better;
B) winning;
C) equal?
(*solution on page 71*)

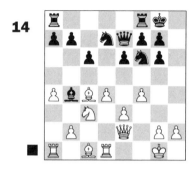

Is Black's position:
A) better;
B) worse;
C) equal?

What should he play:
A) 13...c5;
B) 13...♖fd8;
C) 13...♖ad8 ?
(*solution on page 71*)

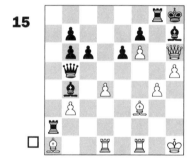

Black's last move was 40...♖a8xa2.
Was this the correct decision?
(*solution on page 72*)

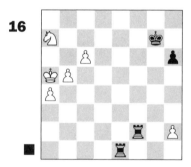

Is Black's position:
A) winning;
B) hopeless;
C) equal?
(*solution on page 72*)

17

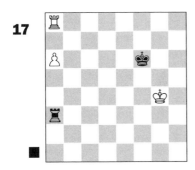

Is Black's position:
  A) equal;
  B) winning?
(solution on page 73)

18

Is White's position:
  A) better;
  B) worse;
  C) equal?
(solution on page 74)

19

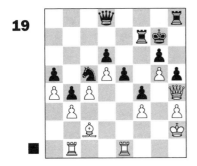

Is Black's position:
  A) better;
  B) worse;
  C) equal?
(solution on page 75)

20

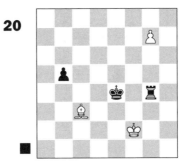

Is Black's position:
  A) winning;
  B) equal?
(solution on page 76)

21

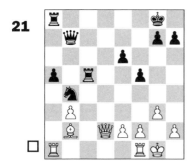

Is White's position:
 A) better;
 B) worse;
 C) equal?
(*solution on page 77*)

22

Is White's position:
 A) better;
 B) slightly better;
 C) equal?
(*solution on page 77*)

23

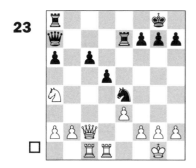

How should White play:
 A) 20.♕xc6;
 B) 20.♘c5 ?
(*solution on page 78*)

24

Is Black's position:
 A) better;
 B) worse;
 C) equal?
(*solution on page 79*)

25

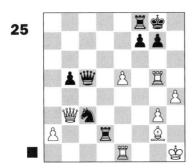

Is Black's position:
 A) better;
 B) winning;
 C) equal?
(solution on page 80)

26

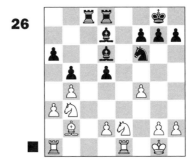

Is Black's position:
 A) better;
 B) worse;
 C) equal?
(solution on page 81)

27

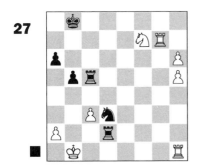

Is White's position:
 A) better;
 B) winning;
 C) equal?
(solution on page 81)

28

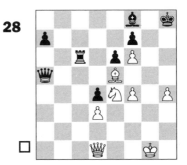

Is White's position:
 A) better;
 B) winning;
 C) equal?
(solution on page 82)

29

Is White's position:
  A) better;
  B) worse;
  C) equal?
(*solution on page 83*)

30

Is Black's position:
  A) winning;
  B) equal?

Can White play 37.♗f3 ?
(*solution on page 84*)

31

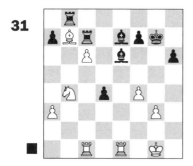

Is Black's position:
  A) better;
  B) worse;
  C) equal?
(*solution on page 85*)

32

Is White's position:
  A) better;
  B) worse;
  C) equal?
(*solution on page 86*)

33

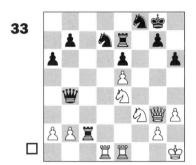

Is White's position:
 A) better;
 B) worse;
 C) winning?
(*solution on page 86*)

34

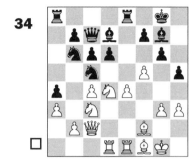

Is White's position:
 A) better;
 B) worse;
 C) equal?
(*solution on page 87*)

35

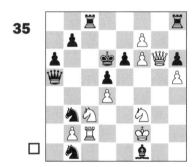

Is White's position:
 A) winning;
 B) lost;
 C) equal?
(*solution on page 87*)

36

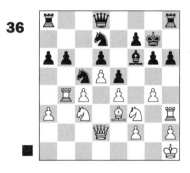

Is Black's position:
 A) better;
 B) worse;
 C) equal?
(*solution on page 88*)

37

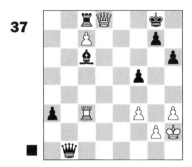

Is Black's position:
A) better;
B) worse;
C) equal?

What should he play:
A) 37...♖xd8;
B) 37...♔h7 ?
(*solution on page 89*)

38

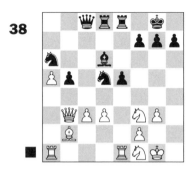

Is Black's position:
A) winning;
B) worse;
C) equal?
(*solution on page 90*)

39

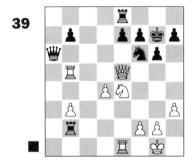

How should Black defend against
the threat of g2-g4-g5 ?
(*solution on page 90*)

40

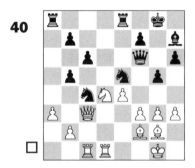

Is White's position:
A) better;
B) worse;
C) equal?

What should he play:
A) 23.♘b3;
B) 23.♔h2;
C) 23.♕c2;
D) 23.b3 ?
(*solution on page 91*)

41

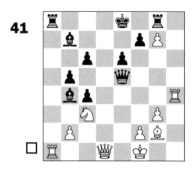

Is White's position:
 A) winning;
 B) equal;
 C) worse?
(solution on page 91)

42

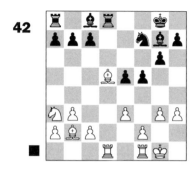

Is Black's position:
 A) better;
 B) worse;
 C) equal?

What should he play:
 A) 15...♖d7;
 B) 15...♖e8;
 C) 15...♖f8 ?
(solution on page 92)

43

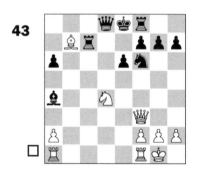

Is White's position:
 A) winning;
 B) equal;
 C) worse?

Can he play 21.♘f5 ?
(solution on page 92)

44

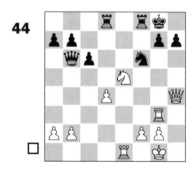

Is White's position:
 A) winning;
 B) equal;
 C) worse?

Can he play 34.♖xg7+ ?
(solution on page 93)

45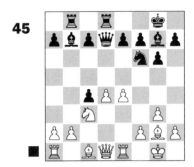

Is Black's position:
A) better;
B) worse;
C) equal?

Can he play 13...♛xd4 ?
(solution on page 94)

46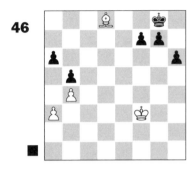

Is Black's position:
A) lost;
B) winning,
C) equal?
(solution on page 94)

47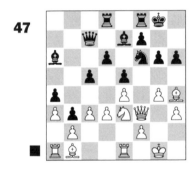

Is Black's position:
A) better;
B) slightly better;
C) worse?
(solution on page 95)

48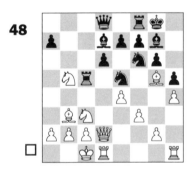

Is White's position:
A) winning;
B) equal;
C) better?
(solution on page 96)

49

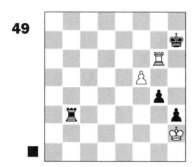

Is Black's position:
 A) equal;
 B) winning?
(solution on page 96)

50

Is White's position:
 A) better;
 B) slightly better;
 C) worse?
(solution on page 97)

51

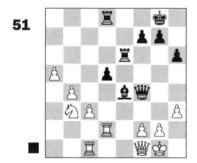

Is Black's position:
 A) winning;
 B) lost;
 C) equal?
(solution on page 98)

52

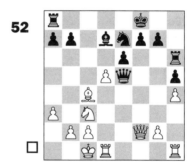

How should White realise his
advantage?
(solution on page 98)

53

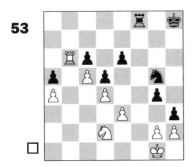

Is White's position:
 A) better;
 B) winning;
 C) equal?
(*solution on page 99*)

54

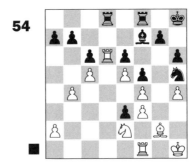

Is Black's position:
 A) better;
 B) worse;
 C) equal?
(*solution on page 99*)

55

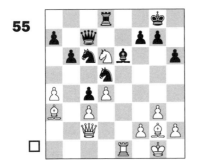

Is White's position:
 A) better;
 B) slightly better?
(*solution on page 100*)

56

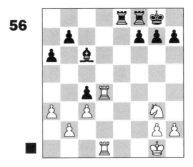

Is Black's position:
 A) better;
 B) winning;
 C) equal?
(*solution on page 101*)

57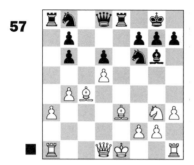

Is Black's position:
A) better;
B) equal;
C) worse?

What should he play:
A) 16...♘h5;
B) 16...♘bd7;
C) 16...♘e4 ?
(solution on page 101)

58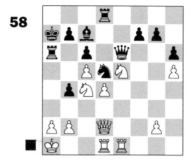

Is Black's position:
A) better;
B) worse;
C) equal?
(solution on page 102)

59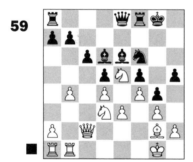

Is Black's position:
A) better;
B) worse;
C) equal?
(solution on page 102)

60

Is White's position:
A) winning;
B) equal;
C) worse?
(solution on page 103)

61

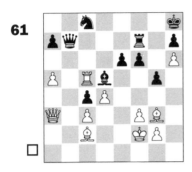

How should White realise his
advantage?
(*solution on page 103*)

62

Here there followed 1...♘cb4. Does
this move:
 A) lose;
 B) equalise;
 C) lead to an advantage for Black?
(*solution on page 104*)

63

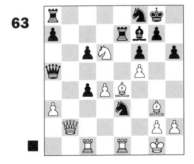

Is Black's position:
 A) better;
 B) worse;
 C) equal?
(*solution on page 104*)

64

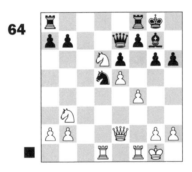

Is Black's position:
 A) better;
 B) worse;
 C) equal?
(*solution on page 105*)

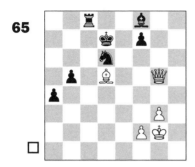

65

How should White continue?
(*solution on page 105*)

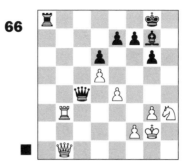

66

Here Black played 33...♖a1.
How should we assess the position
after this move:
  A) drawn;
  B) Black is winning;
  C) White is winning?
(*solution on page 106*)

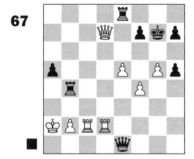

67

Is Black's position:
  A) better;
  B) worse;
  C) equal?
(*solution on page 106*)

68

Is Black's position:
  A) better;
  B) worse;
  C) equal?
(*solution on page 107*)

69

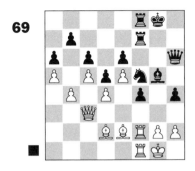

What is the best way for Black to realise his positional advantage?
(*solution on page 107*)

70

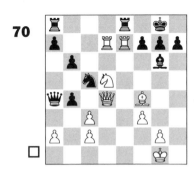

How should White crown his attack?
(*solution on page 108*)

71

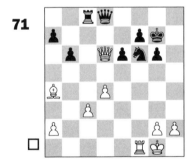

Is White's position:
A) better;
B) worse;
C) equal?
(*solution on page 108*)

72

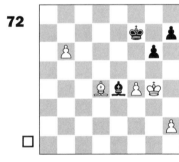

Is White's position:
A) winning;
B) drawn?
(*solution on page 109*)

73

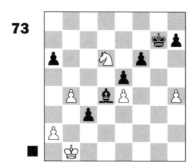

Is Black's position:
 A) better;
 B) worse;
 C) equal?
(solution on page 110)

74

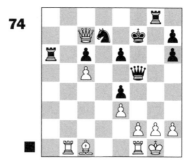

Is Black's position:
 A) better;
 B) worse;
 C) equal?
(solution on page 111)

75

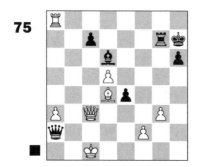

Is Black's position:
 A) better;
 B) worse;
 C) equal?
(solution on page 111)

76

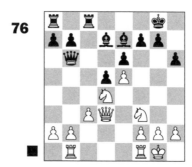

Is Black's position:
 A) better;
 B) worse;
 C) equal?
(solution on page 112)

77

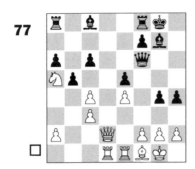

Is White's position:
A) better;
B) worse;
C) equal?
(*solution on page 112*)

78

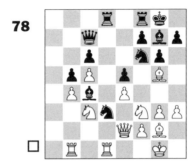

Is White's position:
A) better;
B) worse;
C) equal?
(*solution on page 113*)

79

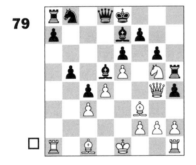

Is White's position:
A) winning;
B) worse;
C) equal?
(*solution on page 114*)

80

Is White's position:
A) better;
B) worse;
C) equal?
(*solution on page 114*)

81

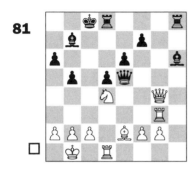

Is White's position:
 A) better;
 B) worse;
 C) equal?
(solution on page 115)

82

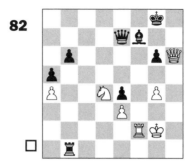

White has sacrificed a pawn, to
ensure his pieces threatening
positions, close to the enemy king.
Was he right?
(solution on page 115)

83

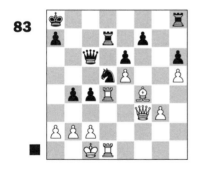

Is Black's position:
 A) better;
 B) worse;
 C) equal?

What should he play:
 A) 31...c3;
 B) 31...♜c8;
 C) 31...♜b7 ?
(solution on page 116)

84

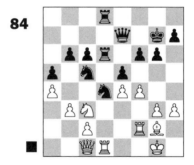

Is Black's position:
 A) better;
 B) winning;
 C) equal?
(solution on page 116)

85

Is Black's position:
 A) better;
 B) slightly better;
 C) equal?
(*solution on page 118*)

86

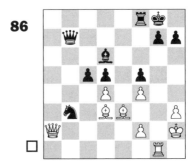

Is White's position:
 A) worse;
 B) slightly worse;
 C) equal?
(*solution on page 118*)

87

Is White's position:
 A) better;
 B) slightly better;
 C) equal?
(*solution on page 119*)

88

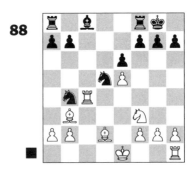

Is Black's position:
 A) better;
 B) equal;
 C) worse?

Should he continue 18...♘d3+ ?
(*solution on page 119*)

89

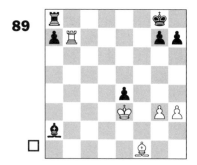

Is White's position:
  A) hopeless;
  B) equal;
  C) worse?
(solution on page 120)

90

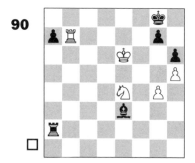

Does White's active king compensate for the pawn minus?
(solution on page 121)

91

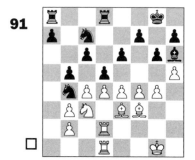

Is White's position:
  A) better;
  B) equal;
  C) worse?
(solution on page 121)

92

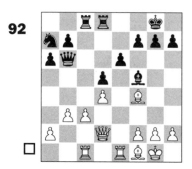

Show a plan of play for White.
(solution on page 122)

93

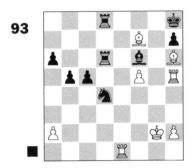

Is Black's position:
 A) worse;
 B) better;
 C) slightly better?
(solution on page 122)

94

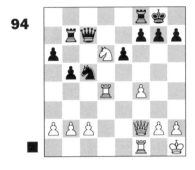

Is Black's position:
 A) better;
 B) equal;
 C) worse?
(solution on page 123)

95

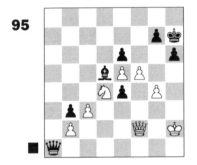

Is Black's position:
 A) better;
 B) equal;
 C) worse?
(solution on page 123)

96

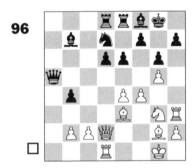

Is White's position:
 A) better;
 B) equal;
 C) worse?
(solution on page 124)

97

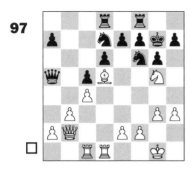

Is White's position:
A) better;
B) equal;
C) worse?
(solution on page 125)

98

Is White's position:
A) better;
B) equal;
C) worse?

Can he play 14.♗xd5 ?
(solution on page 126)

99

Can White save himself?
(solution on page 126)

100

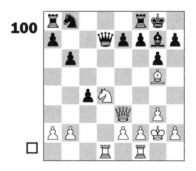

Is White's position:
A) better;
B) equal;
C) worse?

What should he play:
A) 15.♕xe7;
B) 15.♕f3;
C) 15.♕e4 ?
(solution on page 127)

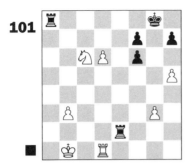

Is Black's position:
  A) hopeless;
  B) winning;
  C) equal?
(*solution on page 127*)

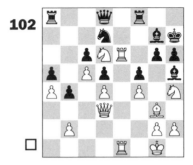

How can White realise his advantage?
(*solution on page 128*)

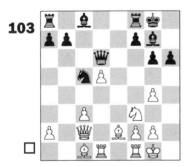

Is White's position:
  A) better;
  B) equal;
  C) worse?
(*solution on page 129*)

Is White's position:
  A) better;
  B) equal;
  C) worse?
(*solution on page 129*)

105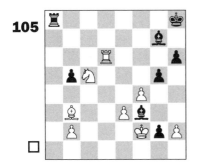

Is White's position:
  A) better;
  B) equal;
  C) hopeless?
(solution on page 130)

106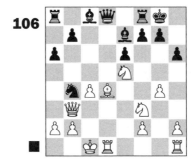

Is Black's position:
  A) better;
  B) equal;
  C) worse?
(solution on page 130)

107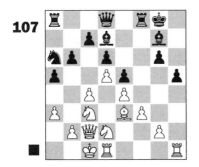

Is Black's position:
  A) better;
  B) equal;
  C) worse?
(solution on page 131)

108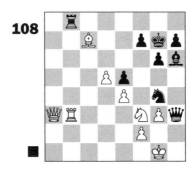

What should Black play?
(solution on page 132)

109

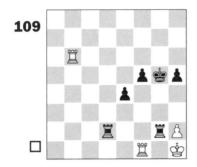

White chose 45.h4+. How should
Black reply:
  A) 45...♔g4;
  B) 45...♔xh4 ?
(solution on page 132)

110

Is White's position:
  A) better;
  B) equal;
  C) worse ?
(solution on page 133)

111

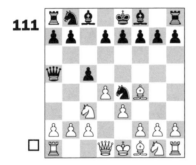

How should White continue:
  A) 6.♗d3;
  B) 6.♘e2 ?
(solution on page 133)

112

Is White's position:
  A) better;
  B) worse;
  C) winning ?
(solution on page 134)

113

Is Black's position:
 A) worse;
 B) better;
 C) equal?

How should he continue:
 A) 21... 0-0-0;
 B) 21...0-0;
 C) 21...♗h3;
 D) 21...f6;
 E) 21...♘c4 ?
(*solution on page 134*)

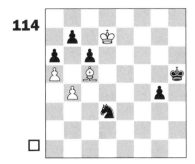

114

Is White's position:
 A) equal;
 B) hopeless?

What should he play:
 A) 68.♗a7;
 B) 68.♗d6;
 C) 68.♗g1 ?
(*solution on page 135*)

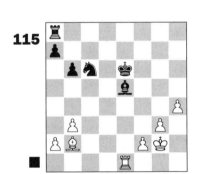

115

Is Black's position:
 A) better;
 B) lost;
 C) equal?

What should he play:
 A) 35...♔f6;
 B) 35...♔f5;
 C) 35...♔d5 ?
(*solution on page 136*)

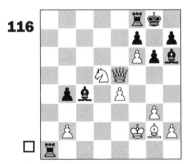

116

Is White's position:
 A) winning;
 B) hopeless;
 C) equal?
(*solution on page 137*)

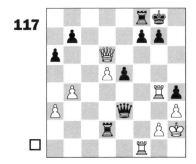

117

Is White's position:
  A) winning;
  B) equal;
  C) worse?
(solution on page 138)

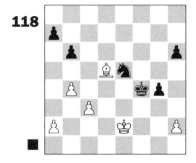

118

Is Black's position:
  A) better;
  B) worse;
  C) equal?
(solution on page 138)

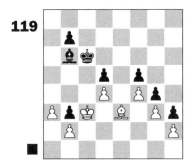

119

Is Black's position:
  A) lost;
  B) equal?
(solution on page 139)

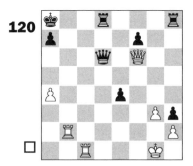

120

Is White's position:
  A) better;
  B) worse;
  C) equal?
(solution on page 140)

121

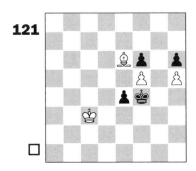

Is White's position:
  A) winning;
  B) equal?
(solution on page 140)

122

Is Black's position:
  A) better;
  B) worse;
  C) equal?

Can he play 29...♗xc5 30.bxc5 ♕xc5 ?
(solution on page 141)

123

Is the continuation 19.♖xb7:
  A) favourable for White;
  B) favourable for Black;
  C) leading to equality?
(solution on page 142)

124

Is White's position:
  A) better;
  B) worse;
  C) equal?
(solution on page 142)

125

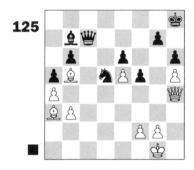

Can Black take the pawn –
39...♕xe5 ?
(*solution on page 143*)

126

Assess Black's position:
  A) better;
  B) winning;
  C) equal;
  D) worse?
(*solution on page 144*)

127

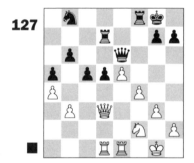

Is Black's position:
  A) better;
  B) worse;
  C) equal?
(*solution on page 144*)

128

What should Black play:
  A) 5...0-0;
  B) 5...d5;
  C) 5...d6 ?
(*solution on page 145*)

129

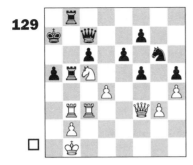

Is White's position:
 A) better;
 B) worse;
 C) winning?
(solution on page 146)

130

Is Black's position:
 A) better;
 B) worse;
 C) equal?
(solution on page 146)

131

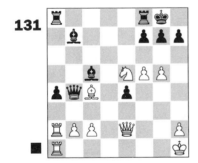

How should Black exploit the strength of his two bishops?
(solution on page 147)

132

What should Black play:
 A) 1...♖c2;
 B) 1...♗e6;
 C) 1...♕b6 ?
(solution on page 147)

133

What should Black play:
 A) 1...♖xd4;
 B) 1...fxe4 ?
(solution on page 147)

134

Can White win the e4-pawn by means of 1.g4 ?
(solution on page 148)

135

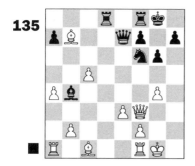

Does Black have sufficient compensation for the sacrificed pawn?

What should he play:
 A) 1...♘xg4;
 B) 1...♗xc5 ?
(solution on page 149)

136

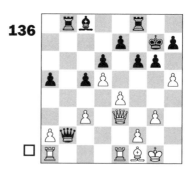

Is White's position:
 A) better;
 B) worse;
 C) equal?
(solution on page 149)

137

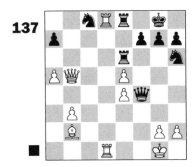

Is Black's position:
  A) winning;
  B) hopeless;
  C) equal?
(solution on page 150)

138

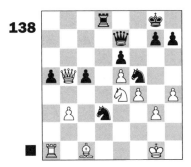

What should Black play:
  A) 1...♘xg3;
  B) 1...h6 ?
(solution on page 150)

139

Is White's position:
  A) winning;
  B) drawn ?
(solution on page 151)

140

Can White exploit his large advantage in development?
(solution on page 152)

141

Is Black's position:
A) better;
B) worse;
C) equal?
(*solution on page 152*)

142

Is Black's position:
A) better;
B) worse;
C) equal?
(*solution on page 153*)

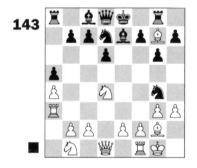

143

Is Black's position:
A) better;
B) worse;
C) equal?

What would you play:
A) 11...♘xf2;
B) 11...♖xg7;
C) 11...♘ge5 ?
(*solution on page 153*)

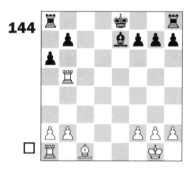

144

Can White take the pawn?
(*solution on page 154*)

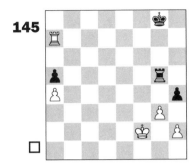

145

Is White's position:
  A) drawn;
  B) winning ?
(solution on page 154)

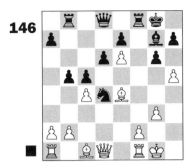

146

Is Black's position:
  A) better;
  B) worse;
  C) equal?
(solution on page 156)

147

Is Black's position:
  A) better;
  B) worse;
  C) equal?
(solution on page 156)

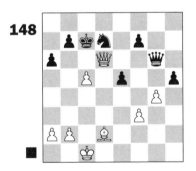

148

Is Black's position:
  A) hopeless;
  B) equal;
  C) better?
(solution on page 157)

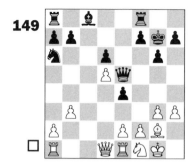

149

Is White's position:
  A) better;
  B) worse;
  C) equal?
(*solution on page 157*)

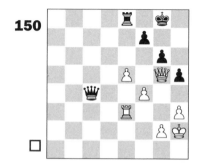

150

Can White exploit his minimal
material advantage?
(*solution on page 158*)

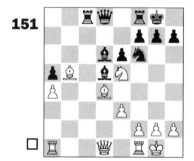

151

White played 1.♕e2, planning,
by means of ♖fc1, to exploit the
weakness of the point c6. Is this
move good?
(*solution on page 158*)

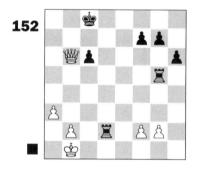

152

Is Black's position:
  A) equal;
  B) winning;
  C) better?
(*solution on page 159*)

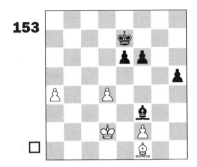

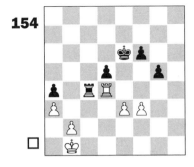

Is White's position:
  A) winning;
  B) equal;
  C) worse?

What should he play:
  A) 1.♔e3;
  B) 1.a5;
  C) 1.♗e2 ?
(solution on page 159)

Is White's position:
  A) equal;
  B) hopeless;
  C) better?
(solution on page 160)

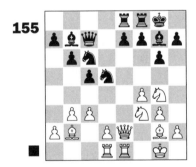

Is Black's position:
  A) better;
  B) worse;
  C) equal?
(solution on page 160)

Is White's position:
  A) better;
  B) equal;
  C) winning?
(solution on page 161)

157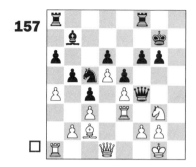

Is White's position:
 A) better;
 B) worse;
 C) equal?
(solution on page 161)

158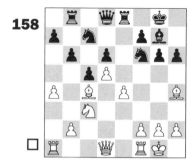

Is White's position:
 A) better;
 B) worse;
 C) equal?
(solution on page 162)

159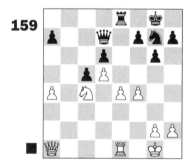

Is Black's position:
 A) better;
 B) worse;
 C) equal?
(solution on page 163)

160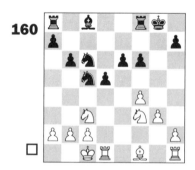

Is White's position:
 A) better;
 B) worse;
 C) equal?
(solution on page 163)

161

Is White's position:
 A) better;
 B) winning;
 C) worse?
(solution on page 164)

162

Is White's position:
 A) better;
 B) worse;
 C) equal?
(solution on page 164)

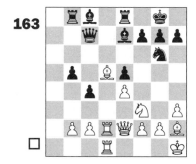

163

Can White play 1.♗xf7+ ?
(solution on page 165)

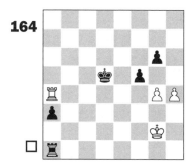

164

Is White's position:
 A) equal;
 B) winning?
(solution on page 165)

165

Is White's position:
  A) better;
  B) worse;
  C) equal?
(solution on page 166)

166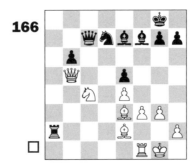

Can White play 25.♘xb6 ?
(solution on page 167)

167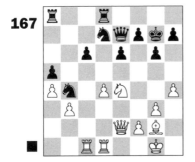

Can Black open the game to his advantage with 24...e5 ?
(solution on page 167)

168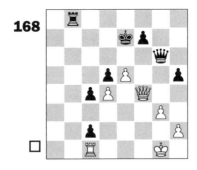

Is White's position:
  A) worse;
  B) equal;
  C) hopeless?
(solution on page 168)

169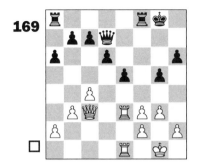

Is White's position:
A) better;
B) worse;
C) equal?
(solution on page 168)

170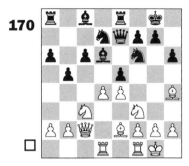

Is White's position:
A) better;
B) worse;
C) equal?
(solution on page 169)

171

Is White's position:
A) better;
B) worse;
C) equal?
(solution on page 169)

172

Is White's position:
A) better;
B) worse;
C) equal?
(solution on page 170)

173

What should Black play:
A) 8...♘h5;
B) 8...♗b7;
C) 8...♘c6 ?
(solution on page 171)

174

Is Black's position:
A) better;
B) worse;
C) equal?
(solution on page 171)

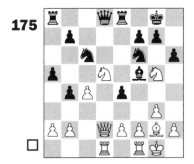

175

White played 18.♕f4. This continuation leads to:
A) an advantage for White;
B) an advantage for Black;
C) an equal position?
(solution on page 172)

176

Is Black's position:
A) better;
B) winning;
C) equal?

What should he play:
A) 48...♗d5;
B) 48...♗e6;
C) 48...♗d3 ?
(solution on page 172)

177

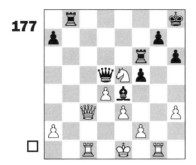

Is White's position:
 A) winning;
 B) better;
 C) worse?
(solution on page 174)

178

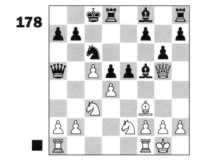

Is Black's position:
 A) better;
 B) winning;
 C) hopeless?
(solution on page 174)

179

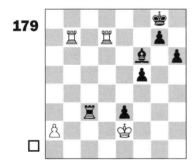

Is White's position:
 A) better;
 B) worse;
 C) equal?
(solution on page 175)

180

Is White's position:
 A) winning;
 B) better;
 C) equal?
(solution on page 176)

181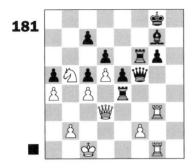

Find the strongest continuation.
(*solution on page 176*)

182

How should White realise his
advantage?
(*solution on page 177*)

183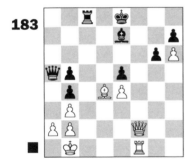

Is Black's position:
  A) better;
  B) worse;
  C) equal?
(*solution on page 177*)

184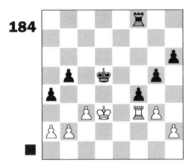

Is Black's position:
  A) winning;
  B) better;
  C) equal?
(*solution on page 178*)

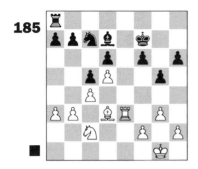

Is Black's position:
  A) better;
  B) worse;
  C) equal?

Which continuation would you prefer:
  A) 29...b5;
  B) 29...♖e8;
  C) 29...f5 ?
(solution on page 179)

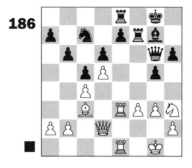

Is Black's position:
  A) better;
  B) worse;
  C) equal?

What would you play:
  A) 23...♗xc3;
  B) 23...e5;
  C) 23...♕h5 ?
(solution on page 179)

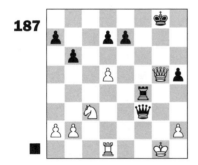

Is Black's position:
  A) equal;
  B) winning;
  C) worse?

What should he play:
  A) 32...♔f7;
  B) 32...♔h7 ?
(solution on page 180)

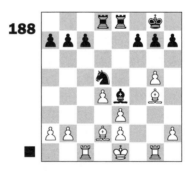

Is Black's position:
  A) better;
  B) worse;
  C) equal?
(solution on page 180)

189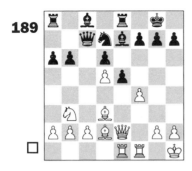

How should White continue?
(*solution on page 181*)

190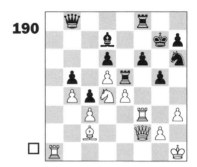

Is White's position:
  A) better;
  B) winning?
(*solution on page 181*)

191

White played 29.♗xd5. This move leads to:
  A) equality;
  B) defeat;
  C) victory?
(*solution on page 182*)

192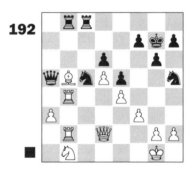

Is Black's position:
  A) better;
  B) worse;
  C) equal?
(*solution on page 182*)

193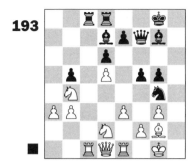

Is Black's position:
A) better;
B) worse;
C) equal?
(solution on page 183)

194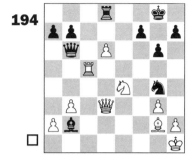

Is White's position:
A) better;
B) worse;
C) equal?

How should he continue:
A) 31.♕c4;
B) 31.♕c2;
C) 31.h3 ?
(solution on page 183)

195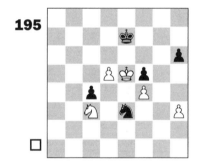

Is White's position:
A) winning;
B) worse;
C) equal?

Assess the continuations:
A) 56.♔d4;
B) 56.♘a4;
C) 56.♘b5;
D) 56.d6+.
(solution on page 184)

196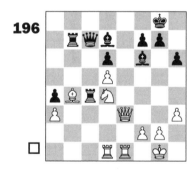

Is White's position:
A) better;
B) worse;
C) equal?
(solution on page 185)

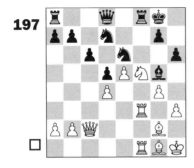

197

How can White realise his
advantage?
(solution on page 185)

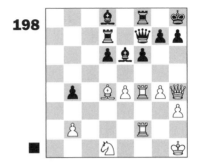

198

Is Black's position:
 A) better;
 B) worse;
 C) equal?
(solution on page 186)

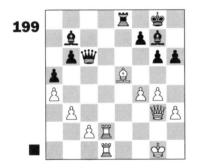

199

Is Black's position:
 A) better;
 B) worse;
 C) equal?
(solution on page 186)

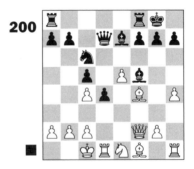

200

Is Black's position:
 A) better;
 B) worse;
 C) equal?
(solution on page 187)

201

Is White's position:
 A) better;
 B) worse;
 C) equal?
(solution on page 187)

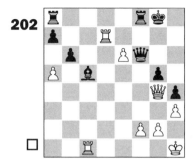

202

Is White's position:
 A) hopeless;
 B) equal;
 C) winning?
(solution on page 188)

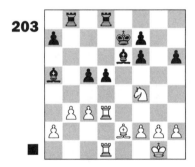

203

Is Black's position:
 A) worse;
 B) hopeless;
 C) equal?
(solution on page 188)

204

Is White's position:
 A) better;
 B) worse;
 C) equal;
 D) unclear?
(solution on page 189)

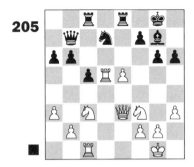

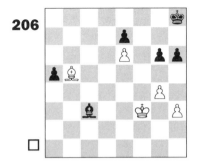

Is Black's position:
 A) better;
 B) worse;
 C) equal?

Is White's position:
 A) equal;
 B) hopeless?
(*solution on page 191*)

What should he play:
 A) 1...♕c7;
 B) 1...♖e7 ?
(*solution on page 190*)

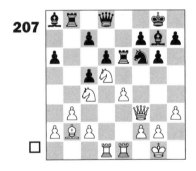

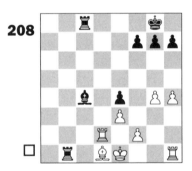

Is White's position:
 A) better;
 B) worse;
 C) equal?

Is White's position:
 A) equal;
 B) worse;
 C) hopeless?
(*solution on page 193*)

What should he play:
 A) 1.♕d3;
 B) 1.♘xf6+;
 C) 1.♘c3 ?
(*solution on page 192*)

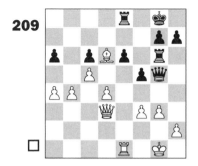

209

Is White's position:
 A) better;
 B) worse;
 C) the game is unclear?
(solution on page 193)

210

Is Black's position:
 A) better;
 B) worse;
 C) equal?
(solution on page 193)

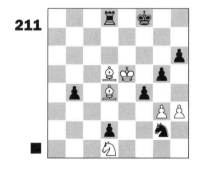

211

Is Black's position:
 A) winning;
 B) better;
 C) equal?

What should he play:
 A) 47...♖xd5+;
 B) 47...♘e3;
 C) 47...♘e1 ?
(solution on page 194)

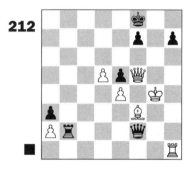

212

Is Black's position:
 A) hopeless;
 B) equal;
 C) better?
(solution on page 195)

213

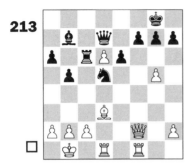

How can White realise his material advantage?
(*solution on page 196*)

214

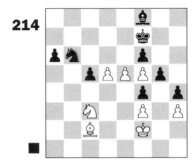

Is Black's position:
  A) winning;
  B) equal;
  C) better?
(*solution on page 196*)

215

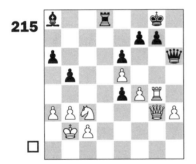

Is White's position:
  A) better;
  B) winning;
  C) equal?
(*solution on page 197*)

216

Is White's position:
  A) better;
  B) worse;
  C) equal?
(*solution on page 198*)

217

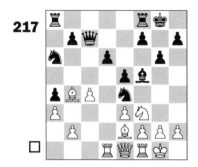

Is White's position:
 A) better;
 B) worse;
 C) equal?
(solution on page 198)

218

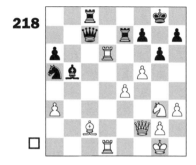

Is White's position:
 A) better;
 B) winning;
 C) equal?
(solution on page 199)

219

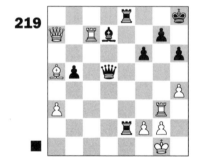

Is Black's position:
 A) better;
 B) worse;
 C) equal?
(solution on page 199)

220

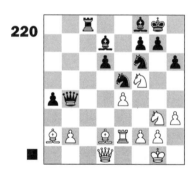

Can Black play 27...♕xb2 ?
(solution on page 199)

221

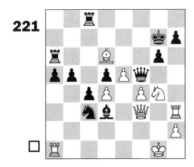

Is White's position:
 A) hopeless;
 B) equal;
 C) winning?
(solution on page 200)

222

Is White's position:
 A) winning;
 B) better;
 C) equal?
(solution on page 200)

223

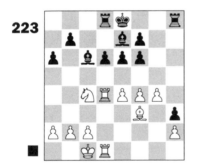

Is Black's position:
 A) better;
 B) worse;
 C) equal?
(solution on page 201)

224

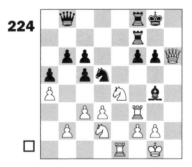

Is White's position:
 A) better;
 B) worse;
 C) equal?
(solution on page 201)

Solutions

Solution 1

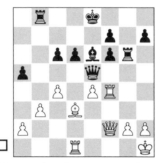

Thanks to the disconnected enemy forces and the weakened position of his king, White has a large advantage. An uncastled king usually becomes a good object of attack. In the game L.Guliev-Aroshidze (Adana 2006) followed
22.♖f5!
Winning an important tempo for the queen to break through into the enemy camp. It is clear that the position is hopeless after 22...♗xf5 23.exf5, and if the rook retreats, White decides things with ♖e1.
22...♕c3 23.♕a7 ♖c8 24.♕xa5 ♕b2
Of course, exchanging queens and heading to the endgame is hardly to Black's taste.
25.♖d2 ♕d4 26.♖ff2 ♖g5 27.♕a3 ♖h5 28.♗f1 ♕xe4 29.♕xd6
And White's advantage is close to decisive.

Conclusion: If the enemy king is stuck in the centre, try to open central lines.

The game was lost because, at a certain moment, the defender was unable to keep up with his opponent in the speed of regrouping his forces. – Aron Nimzowitsch

Solution 2

A minute weakness can sometimes take over one's mind! In chess, this can be very costly. Here Black should have played **12...♘e8** or **12...♕e7**, defending the d6-pawn and retaining a satisfactory position.
In the game S.Guliev-Nikitin (Voroshilovgrad 1989) Black did not want to settle for a quiet defence and instead chose an 'active' move:
12...♘b6?
but after
13.♘xd6! ♗g4 14.a5 ♕xd6 15.♗f4 ♕d8 16.♗xb8 ♕xb8 17.axb6
White had a winning position.

Conclusion: Look carefully for possibilities of establishing a pin!

In nature, the opposite causes often produce the same actions: the horse equally falls to the ground from stagnation and from being driven excessively. – Mikhail Lermontov

Solution 3

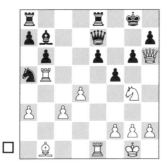

In the game Tkachenko-S.Guliev (Voroshilovgrad 1989) Black had been forced for a long time to conduct a difficult defence, due to the weakness of the dark squares on the kingside. Here, he decided that the time had come for active operations and he played 23...f7-f5. At first glance, he seems right, since if the knight retreats, Black takes over the initiative. However, all the white pieces are very actively placed and this allows him to go over to an energetic attack! White has a winning position.
After
24.♗xf5! gxf5 25.♘f6+ ♚h8 26.♖xe6!
Black resigned. The pawn protection around the black king was seriously compromised. This allowed White to carry out a strong attack. One recalls Iosif Brodsky's words:

From the position of the pawns, one can guess the state of the king.

Conclusion: A weakened king position is a serious combinational motif!

Solution 4

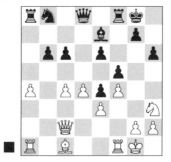

In reality, it is not so easy to assess this position. Both sides have some poorly-placed pieces and pawn weaknesses. Delving deeply into the essence of the position, one can see that Black's pieces are closer to the centre, whilst the white centre is vulnerable. In addition, it is Black's move. This allows us to conclude that Black stands better.
The game Kakageldiev-S.Guliev (Ashkabad 1989) continued
18...c5! 19.♖d1 cxd4 20.exd4 ♘c6 21.♗e3 ♗f6
Stronger was 21...♕d7!, and Black is better.
22.♖ab1 ♘a5 23.♕a2
It was worth considering 23.c5 with complicated play.
23...♖c8 24.♖bc1 ♖f7!
And Black's advantage assumed real proportions.

Conclusion: Mobility of the centre is the source of tension.

Find the opponent's weak spot and strike while the iron is hot! – Vlastimil Hort, Vlastimil Jansa

Solution 5

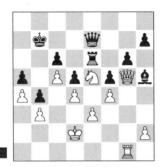

White has a very strong knight on e5 and Black also has a bad bishop, but the black position is not easy to break down.

With patience, Black could hold the draw. With this aim, he should have played **46...♔c7!**. It is not obvious how the lovely-looking knight can demonstrate its superiority over the bad bishop. The position is equal. However, in the game Komarov-S. Guliev (Soviet Union tt-jr 1989) Black, tired of waiting tactics, decided to change the position by exchanging queens.

46...♕xg5?

However, this was a very serious mistake, and after

47.fxg5!

White obtained access to the important f4-square. Black underestimated the importance of this square for the outcome of the game. He paid dearly for this:

47...♔c7 48.♘d3 ♖e4 49.♘f4 ♔d7

Or 49...♖xf4 50.exf4 ♔d7 51.♖g3 and then ♖e3 followed by h2-h3, after which Black inevitably falls into zugzwang and must allow the rook into his camp.

50.♖g3 ♗g4 51.♘d3 ♗h5 52.♖h3 ♔e6 53.♘f2 ♔e7 54.♘xe4 dxe4 55.♔e1 ♔e6 56.♖h4 ♔d5 57.♔d2

♔e6 58.♔c2 ♔d5 59.♔c1 ♔e6 60.♔d2 ♔d5 61.♔e1 ♔e6 62.h3 ♔d5

White gains time with the repetition of moves.

63.♖f4 ♔e6 64.♖f1 ♔d5 65.♖f2 ♔e6 66.d5+

And Black resigned.

Conclusion: Patience, patience and, for the third time, patience!

He who is not in a hurry to get somewhere, gets there. – Mikhail Bulgakov

Solution 6

The major pieces on the second rank create decisive threats.

White's last hope was to sacrifice the bishop, so as to draw the black king into the open and hope to give perpetual check.

However, accurate calculation of the variations shows that Black is winning. But to achieve this, the black king must march through the enemy camp – only there can he breathe easily and support the attack by his own forces.

The road by which the black king must travel is under heavy fire from the white pieces and so Black must play exceptionally precisely.

1...♔xg6 2.♕c6+ ♔g5

Nothing is changed by 2...♔h7 3.♕e4+ ♔h8 4.♕a8+.

3.♖xe5+ ♔h4 4.♕h6+ ♘h5!

Black had to see this move in advance; after 4...♔g3? 5.♖e3+ White wins.

5.♕g5+

He loses after 5.♕xh5+ ♔g3 or 5.♖xh5+ ♔g3.

5...♔xh3 6.♖e3+ ♕xe3!

This is very nice, but he also wins with the prosaic 6...♘g3+ 7.♖xg3+ ♔xg3 (7...♕xg3? 8.♕xd2) 8.♕e5+ ♕f4 etc.

7.♕xe3+ ♘g3+

However, in the game Allahverdiyev-L.Guliev (Baku 1991) Black at first did not believe his eyes: 2...♔h7 (instead of 2...♔g5) 3.♕e4+ ♔g8 4.♕a8+ ♔f7 5.♕b7+ ♔g6 6.♕c6+ and only here he found 6...♔g5!. The game went on along the lines shown above.

Conclusion: You should believe your own eyes!

Solution 7

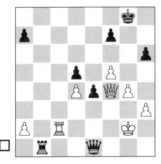

Both king positions are dubious. Black's threats look decisive, but it is White to play, and he exploits to the full the compromised pawn position around the black king. The position is a draw.

In the game S.Guliev-Nevednichy (Soviet Union tt 1991) there followed

42.♖c8+ ♔h7

Completely bad is 42...♔g7? 43.f6+ ♔h7 44.♖h8+! ♔xh8 45.♕xh6+, mating.

43.♖h8+!

And here, in view of the variation 43...♔xh8 44.♕xh6+ ♔g8 45.♕g5+ ♔f8 46.♕d8+ the players agreed a draw.

Conclusion: The best defence is counterattack!

Great desperation always generates great strength. – Stefan Zweig

Solution 8

Not a very standard position, you'll agree! The correct answer is that White stands better: **15.cxb6! ♗xa3** (15...♗g5 16.b7) **16.b7 ♗xb7 17.♖xb7 ♘c5 18.♘xc5 ♗xc5 19.♗xh5 ♖xh5 20.♕f3 ♖h7 21.♖fb1** (the immediate 21.♘a4 is also possible) and then ♘a4 followed by c4-c5 promises White a large advantage. If you missed this zwischenzug, do not despair. You are not alone – in the game S.Guliev-Godes (Baku 1991) White played

15.♕xc1

and only then noticed the above-mentioned possibility.

Conclusion: It is not always necessary to capture the more valuable piece!

It is well known that the famous trainer Vladimir Zak often used to test his pupils with exercises involving zwischenzugs, to test their alertness and ingenuity.

Solution 9

At first glance the position looks equal, but in fact White is winning! In the game Kharlov-S.Guliev (Chelyabinsk 1991) White exploited the bad position of the enemy pieces and, by a rapid march of the d-pawn, decided the game in his favour.
23.d5! ♗f5 24.d6!
And Black resigned. After 24...♕xd6 25.♖ad1 White wins at least a piece.

We find ourselves in a weeping state, when we have no space to ourselves. – Tofiq Bahramov

Conclusion: During a game, each piece's influence should not extend beyond that piece's capabilities. Otherwise, an overload can arise

or the piece can find itself too far away to return to the key area when the need arises. Both can be good motifs for a combination.

You can't keep two watermelons in one hand! (Azeri proverb)

Solution 10

Despite the fact that the game has only just begun, accuracy is already required of Black. In the game Belov-S.Guliev (Katovice 1991) Black failed to appreciate the seriousness of the moment and played:
6...♞f6?
After
7.cxd5! exd5 8.♗xf6 gxf6
(necessary, because after 8...♕xf6 there follows 9.♞xd5, winning a pawn)
9.e3
he found himself in an unenviable position.
With the careful **6...♞e7!** Black's position would have been somewhat passive, but perfectly playable.

Conclusion: Carelessness is often punished!

A good start is not a trifle, but begins with trifles. – Socrates

Solution 11

Both sides have completed their development, but neither can be too happy at the position of their queen. It is White's move and he finds a better location for the queen, one which guarantees him an advantage.

13.♕a3! cxd4

The continuation 13...b6 14.♘g5! e5 15.e4! (stronger than 15.dxe5 ♘xe5 16.♖ad1 ♕c6 17.♗xe5 ♗xe5 18.♗f3 ♕a4! with complicated play) 15...♕d6 16.♗c4 ♗e8 17.dxc5 ♕xc5 18.♕xc5 bxc5 19.♗e3 or 13...c4 14.♘d2 is in White's favour.

14.cxd4 ♖dc8

14...♕a5? 15.♕xa5 ♘xa5 16.♗c7.

15.♖fc1 ♕a5 16.♕b3 ♘b4

Weak was 16...♕b4? because of 17.♖xc6, but more tenacious was 16...♕b6!?.

17.♗c4! e6 18.♗d6!

And White obtained the advantage. This was the game S.Guliev-Schmuter (Moscow 1991).

Conclusion: The eternal refrain of all chess players is: do not have bad pieces!

If one piece stands badly, the whole game is bad. – Siegbert Tarrasch

Solution 12

This is one of those positions which are hard to judge. White has a protected passed pawn, but a weak king. Black has a weak back rank and e5-pawn. Which of these factors will prove the most important? In fact, Black has a decisive advantage. By exploiting the exposed white king position, with the aid of zigzag manoeuvres by his queen, he wins and a pawn and gradually realises it.

The game Gross-S.Guliev (Ceske Budejovice 1992) continued:

27...♕e3+ 28.♔g2 ♕d2+ 29.♔g1 ♕d4+ 30.♔g2 ♕xb2+ 31.♔g1 ♕d4+ 32.♔g2 ♕b2+ 33.♔g1 ♖g8!

The exchange of rooks favours White and, with his d5-pawn and the insecure position of the black king, he would not stand worse.

34.♖d1 ♕xa2 35.d6 ♕f7 36.d7 ♖d8 37.♖d6 h6 38.♕d1 c4

And White soon resigned.

Conclusion: Chess is not draughts (checkers), and capturing is not compulsory. Sometimes it is useful to avoid exchanges.

Assessing a position is like using scales. – Mikhail Tal

Solution 13

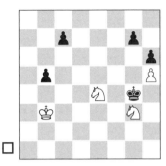

The non-standard material balance makes an exact assessment of the position difficult. But deep calculation of the variations shows that White is winning. Black's task is to eliminate the h5-pawn and to give up his pawns, achieving a theoretically drawn ending of 2♘s vs ♔. However, the course of the game L.Guliev-Rzaev (Baku 1992) showed that Black cannot achieve this. Firstly, White neutralises the enemy queenside pawns.

1.♔b4! c6

If 1...♔f4 2.♔xb5 ♔e5 3.♔c6 ♔e6 4.♔xc7 ♔f7 5.♔d7 (5.♘d6 is also good) 5...g6 6.♔d6 gxh5 7.♘xh5 ♔g6 8.♘eg3 White reaches a theoretically winning position.

2.♔c5 ♔f4 3.♔d6!

After 3.♔xc6?! b4 the game gets sharper, because the white knights must defend one another and the b-pawn can become dangerous. But 3.♔d4! deserves serious consideration. The analysis of this move could fill more than one page, and can serve as independent work for the interested reader. In the process, he will encounter many interesting ideas, typical of such endings, which are well-known to us from the work of Alexey Troitzky.

3...b4 4.♔e6

White's aim is to dodge the black king and eliminate the kingside pawns, thereby bringing his h-pawn to life.

4...c5

After 4...b3 5.♔f7 b2 6.♘c3! ♔xg3 7.♔xg7 ♔f3 8.♔xh6 White wins, thanks to the fact that the black king cannot help his passed pawn. On the board we have an example of the knights creating a barrier – as soon as the king tries to approach the ♘c3, there is a fork, winning the b2-pawn.

5.♔f7 c4 6.♔xg7 c3 7.♔xh6 c2 8.♘c5!

Also possible was 8.♘d2.

8...♔xg3 9.♘b3 ♔f2 10.♔g5! ♔e3 11.h6 ♔d3 12.h7 ♔c3 13.h8♕+

Less clear was 13.♘c1 ♔d2.

13...♔xb3 14.♕a1! ♔c4 15.♔f4 ♔d3 16.♕c1 b3 17.♕e3+ ♔c4 18.♕d2 1-0

Conclusion: It is useful to study standard endgame positions!

Solution 14

White has two bishops and more space. He also controls the centre. In view of all this, it is not difficult to conclude that White stands better. Evidently, Black allowed these unpleasant facts to drive him to a certain degree of panic. He played:

13...c5?

This activity is out of place and allows White to carry out a standard tactical manoeuvre, which brings him a large advantage. The game S.Guliev-Mitura (Karvina 1992) continued:

14.♘a2! ♗a5

A) White is better after 14...a5 15.♘xb4 axb4 16.e4! cxd4 17.e5 ♘d5 (no better is 17...♕c5 18.♕d3 ♘b6 19.♗xe6 fxe6 20.exf6 with advantage) 18.♗xd5 exd5 19.♖xd4;

B) More tenacious was 14...cxd4!?, although even here, after 15.♘xb4 ♕xb4 16.♖xd4 White ensures himself a large advantage.

15.dxc5! e5

Black's problems are not solved by either 15...♘xc5 16.b4!, or 15...♕xc5 16.b4! ♗xb4 17.♘xb4 ♕xb4 18.♗a3.

16.b4 ♗c7 17.a5+−

In the initial position, Black should have stuck to waiting tactics and played **13...♖fd8** or **13...♖ad8**.

Conclusion: Active operations are dangerous in a passive position.

Development is a guiding principle until the end of the game; inexperienced players forget about it even in the opening. – Aron Nimzowitsch

Solution 15

Yes! At first sight, in the game Godes-S.Guliev (Orel 1992) Black had overlooked

41.♗e4

with mating threats. In reality, he had calculated further.

41...♖h2+! 42.♔xh2 ♕e2+ 43.♗g2 ♖xg4 44.♕g7+ ♖xg7 45.fxg7+ ♔g8 46.♔g1 ♗c2

And soon White resigned.

Conclusion: Small boats are comfortable in small reservoirs, but big boats only in big ones. Only there can they manoeuvre properly. The same is true of rooks – to demonstrate their full possibilities, they need open lines, and bishops need open diagonals.

Moderation is essential and doubts useful. – Gustav Mann

Solution 16

Black has a large material advantage, but White has three connected and far-advanced passed pawns.

The game Bednar-S.Guliev (Ostrava 1992) ended in a quick victory for White. Black did not manage to put up anything against the powerful infantry march.

49...♖xh2 50.c7 ♖c2 51.c8♕

51.b6!.
51...♖xc8 52.♘xc8 ♖e8 53.♘d6 ♖a8+ 54.♔b4 ♔f6 55.b6 ♔e6 56.b7 ♖b8 57.♔c5 ♔d7 58.a5 h5 59.a6 ♖xb7 60.axb7 ♔c7 61.♔d5 1-0
At first glance, it is all logical. But even so, the question arises: did Black use all his defensive resources? Let us try to see.

analysis diagram

52...h5!? (52...♖e5!) 53.b6! (53.♘d6 h4! 54.♘f5+ ♔f6 55.♘xh4 ♖e4! 56.♘f3 ♖f4 57.♘d2 ♔e6 58.b6 ♔d7 59.♔b5 ♔c8 60.a5 ♔b8 61.♘c4 ♖f1=) 53...♖b1 (necessary; 53...h4 54.b7 ♖b1 55.♘b6 loses at once) 54.♘d6 (a draw results from 54.♔a6 h4 55.b7 h3 56.♘d6 (56.♘b6 h2) 56...h2 57.♘f5+ ♔f6 58.♘g3 ♔e5 59.♔a7 ♔d6 60.b8♕+ ♖xb8 61.♔xb8 ♔c5) 54... h4 (or 54...♔f6 55.b7! ♖xb7 56.♘xb7 h4 57.♘d6; nor is he saved by 55...h4 56.♘b5) 55.♘f5+ ♔f6 56.♘xh4 ♔e6!? (56...♖b3 57.♔a6 ♖b4 58.a5 ♖xh4 59.b7 ♖b4 60.♔a7, and the black king is not in time) 57.♔a6 ♖b4 58.a5 and White wins. Not winning is 57.♘g6, because after 57...♔d7 58.♔a6, Black has 58...♖e1!, securing a draw. The second main question is: what if Black plays **49...♖c1**, stopping the advance of the c-pawn immediately? **50.b6 ♖c5+ 51.♔a6 ♖a2 52.c7 ♖xa4+ 53.♔b7 ♖ac4=**.

Thus, the diagram position is equal.

Conclusion: The pawn is distinguished from other units in that it cannot move backwards, but also in that it promotes to another piece, once it reaches the eighth rank. This is one of the most important moments in a game of chess.

If your pawn advances 9 squares, you will be hard to beat! – Nizami Gianjavi

In the days of Nizami Gianjavi (the 12th century), it was believed that chess was played on a board measuring 10x10. Therefore, in his poem, the pawn advances not 7 squares but 9. Today, among the researchers, there is no unanimous agreement about the two 'extra' pieces that the players had in the initial position. However, it is clear that even at that time, the rule of pawn promotion existed, contrary to the conclusions of some specialists, that this rule was invented in the Middle Ages in Europe.

Solution 17

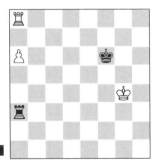

If you are familiar with the studies by Vancura and Romanovsky, devoted to such positions, then you will find the solution easily! The position is drawn. As is well known from endgame textbooks, if Black has ♔g7 and his ♖ on the a-file, whilst White has ♖a8 and pawn on a6, then with the white king anywhere on the squares d2, e2, f2, g2, h2, e3, f3, g3, h3, f4, g4, h4, f5, g5, h5 and e6, Black to move draws easily. In many books, these squares are specifically described as the 'drawing zone'.

Thus, Black should play **54...♔g7!**, and White cannot leave the drawing zone. This is demonstrated by the following variations: 55.♔f5 ♖a5+

analysis diagram

A) 56.♔e6 ♖h5! (for a long time, this manoeuvre was not known about and so the e6-square was not counted as part of the drawing zone, but Romanovsky's discovery dotted the final 'i') 57.♖a7+ ♔g8 58.♖f7 ♖a5 59.♖a7 ♖h5!= etc.; or

B) 56.♔e4 ♖b5 (with the idea of ...♖b6) 57.♖a7+ ♔g6 58.♖b7 ♖a5 59.a7 ♔f6 60.♔d4 ♔e6 61.♔c4 ♔d6 62.♔b4 ♔c6, which also leads to a draw. However, because the white king is quite deep in the drawing zone, Black can permit himself some waiting moves on the a-file. But in the game Babula-S.Guliev (Stare Mesto 1992) Black failed to

cope with this relatively simple situation.

54...♖a1?!

Not yet missing the draw, but a serious step in the wrong direction. This shows that Black has lost the thread of the game.

55.♔f4 ♔g7??

This is losing! Essential was 55...♖a4+. The variation 56.♔e3 ♔g7 57.♔d3 ♖f4 (57...♖b4!?) 58.♖b8 (58.♖a7+ ♔g6!; 58.♔c3 ♖f6 59.♔b4 ♖f4+=) 58...♖a4 59.♖b6 (59.♖b7+ ♔f6 60.a7 ♔e6 61.♔c3 ♖a1 62.♔b4 ♔d6 63.♔b5 ♖b1+=) 59...♔f7 60.♔c3 ♔e7 61.♔b3 ♖a1 62.♔b4 ♔d7 63.♔b5 ♔c7 leads to the well-known Vancura draw.

56.♔e5 ♖f1 57.♖a7+ ♔g6 58.♖b7 ♖f5+ 59.♔d4 ♖a5 60.a7 ♔f6 61.♔c4 ♔e6 62.♔b4 1-0

Conclusion: Just because only a small amount of material remains on the board, this does not mean that the position is easy!

A person who incorrectly fastens his top button is already improperly dressed. – Johann Wolfgang von Goethe

Solution 18

A very non-standard position. White has an extra exchange, but in return,

Black has two pawns for it and is ready to take a third. This will leave him with three passed pawns! But with a detailed examination, one is struck by the scattered position of the black forces and the fact that his king position is not very secure. If White manages to exploit these factors without loss of time, he will have fully-fledged counterplay. However, if Black succeeds in consolidating then White faces serious trouble! Obviously not 37.♖xf2?? ♖c1 mate. White should in the first instance concentrate his attention on 37.b4 or 37.♔b1. If 37.♔b1 ♗e3 38.♖e7 ♖f5 39.♖xf5 gxf5 40.♖xa7 f4 41.♔c2 f3 42.♔d3 f2 43.♔e2

analysis diagram

43...♔g6 44.♖d7 f6 45.gxf6 ♔xf6 Black has sufficient counterplay. In the game S.Guliev-Spassky (Teheran 1992) White chose the more energetic
37.b4!?
As the course of the game showed, Black has nothing to fear here, either.
37...♖f5!
37...♖c2?! 38.♔b1 d3 39.♖d8 ♖d2 40.b5! and Black is in zugzwang.
38.♔b1
38.♔b2? d3 39.♔b3 ♖f3! 40.♔c4 d2–+.

38...a5! 39.bxa5 bxa5 40.♔c2 ♖c5+ 41.♔b3 ♗e3 42.♖e7 ♖f5 43.♖xf5 gxf5 44.♖e5 ♗d2 45.♖xf5 ♔g6! 46.♖f6+ 46.♖d5 ♗c3 47.♔c4 f6=.
46...♔xg5 47.♖xf7 ♗c3 48.♔c4 ♔g4 49.♔d3 ♔g3 50.♔e4 ♗b2 51.♖f3+ ♔g2
And the players agreed a draw. As we see, all analyses and the game itself end in a draw.
That would be it, but for one important point. In my book *Ot Candidata do Grossmeistera* the commentary to this game mistakenly assessed as better for White the position after 43.♔e2 (in the variation 37.♔b1). I take this opportunity to correct this error and apologise to my readers.

Conclusion: Repetition is the mother of learning!

So as to avoid mistakes, you need experience, and to acquire experience, you have to make mistakes. – L.Peter

Solution 19

Those with a subtle positional feeling will have no trouble determining that Black has a clear positional advantage! The excellent knight on c5 dominates the position. But the position is not quite open. If White manages to play ♕h4-f2 and then h3-h4, then he only needs to play ♖e1-e4 (or ♗c2-e4) to complete his fortress. Therefore, Black needs to exploit his positional trumps in short order. He appears to have two possibilities:

A) 1...♖hf8 and then ...♖f5, offering an exchange sacrifice. If White refuses, Black can gradually prepare ...e5-e4;

B) Start immediately with the break ...e5-e4.

In the game Hakpur-S.Guliev (Teheran 1992) Black chose the second path:

1...e4!

and after

2.♗xe4

(2.fxe4 ♘d7!)

2...♖e8 3.♗c2 ♖fe7

he had a large advantage.

Conclusion: In closed positions, a knight is generally stronger than a bishop.

A positional pawn sacrifice is often the best idea, so do not be afraid to decide on it. – Vlastimil Hort, Vlastimil Jansa

Solution 20

The position looks simple, but this simplicity is deceptive. The limited material and far-advanced passed pawn on g7 promise White serious drawing chances. In addition, rook versus bishop with no pawns is generally drawn, apart from a few rare exceptions. Therefore Black needs to keep the b5-pawn, but thanks to his active pieces, he is able to win nonetheless.

1...♖g6!

White is in zugzwang. He has to allow the advance of the b-pawn or worsen the position of his king. He chooses the latter.

2.♔e2 ♖g2+ 3.♔f1 ♔f3 4.♗d4

He also loses after 4.♔e1 ♔e3 5.♔f1 ♖g6 and 4.♗f6 b4 5.♔e1 ♔e3 6.♔d1 ♔d3 7.♔c1 ♔c4 8.♗e5 ♔b3 9.♗d4 ♔a2 10.♔d1 b3 11.♔c1 ♖g6 12.♔d2 (12.♗e5 ♖c6+ 13.♔d2 ♖c8) 12...b2 also leads to a win for Black.

4...b4 5.♔e1

And now in the game Ibragimov-L. Guliev (Baku 1993) Black, instead of 5...♔e4! 6.♗f6 ♔d3 7.♔f1 ♖g6 8.♗e5 b3 9.♔f2 ♔c2 10.♔f3 b2−+ etc., played

5...b3?

and after

6.♔d1 ♔e4 7.♗f6 ♔d3 8.♔c1

a theoretically drawn position was reached. Interestingly, it is even drawn without the g7-pawn. In playing endings, a knowledge of standard positions is very useful. In conditions of limited time, they act as a beacon for the player. Black's haste to advance the b-pawn cost him the win in this game.

Conclusion: Never hurry in taking decisions in a game.

Haste makes waste! (English proverb)

Solution 21

The black king position is weakened. White is better. Here there followed a 'small combination' in the style of Capablanca.
24.♗xg7!
White wins at least a pawn. In the game S.Guliev-Moskalenko (Nikolaev 1993) there followed:
24...♖c2
24...♔xg7 25.♕d4+ is totally bad, whilst after 24...♕xg7 25.♕xb4! axb4 26.♖xa8+ ♔f7 27.♖a7+ ♔f6 28.♖xg7 ♔xg7 29.♖d1 White has an extra pawn in the rook ending and good winning chances.
25.♕d4 ♖xe2?
More tenacious is 25...♕xg7 26.♕xb4 axb4 27.♖xa8+ ♔f7 28.♖a7+ ♔f6 29.♖xg7 ♔xg7 30.♖d1 ♖xe2 31.♖d4 ♔f6 (31...♖e4? 32.♖xe4

fxe4 33.♔f1 ♔f6 34.♔e2 ♔e5 35.♔e3) 32.♖xb4 ♖b2 33.♖b7, and in the rook ending, despite being a pawn down, Black retains drawing chances. Now the weak position of the black king makes itself felt.
26.♗h6 ♘c6 27.♕f6 ♕f7 28.♕c3 ♕b7 29.♖fe1 ♖xe1+ 30.♖xe1 ♖e8 31.♖d1
With a decisive advantage to White.

Conclusion: Never forget about geometrical motifs!

Everything is in the moment. It determines life. – Franz Kafka

Solution 22

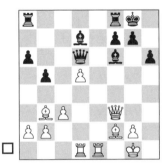

The active positioning of his pieces and also the strong pawn on d5 ensure White a large advantage. In the game L.Guliev-Shabanov (Baku 1993) White correctly assessed the position and, recognising that his advantage was of a dynamic character, realised this was the time to begin combinative play.
1.♖e6!! ♗xe6
Forced; completely bad is 1...fxe6 2.dxe6 ♕xe6 3.♖xd7 or 1...♕c7 2.♖xf6.
2.dxe6 ♕c7 3.exf7+ ♔h8 4.♖e1?!
This is not a mistake, but he could have decided things immediately

with 4.♕e4! followed by ♗c2. Worse is 4.♕f5 ♖xf7 5.♗c2 g5! with unclear play.

4...♖ad8 5.♕h5 ♗g5

5...♕f4 6.♗c5.

6.♕g6 ♖d2 7.♖e8 ♗e7

8.♕e4?!

A) He wins easily after 8.♗c2! ♖xc2 9.♕xc2 ♗c5 (9...♕d7 10.♗d4 ♖xe8 11.♕g6) 10.♗xc5 ♕xc5+ 11.♕f2 ♕d6 12.♕d4+−;

B) Also good is 8.♗e3 ♖e2 9.♗d4!.

8...♗c5 9.♗e3?

9.♗d4!.

9...♖xb2 10.♕d4?? ♕g3 11.♖xf8+ ♗xf8 12.♗f2 ♖b1+ 13.♗d1 ♕d6

And it is Black who has a winning position! White missed several chances to end the game.

To some extent, this lapse may be explained by time-trouble, but as Alekhine said in relation to his game against Tylor (Nottingham 1936):

A chess master's inability to handle the clock is no more of a valid excuse than that of a criminal who claims he was drunk when he committed the offence.

White's play was very strong and creative, but he did not manage to finish things off. At a certain moment, he needed to play

combinatively and go over to the realisation of his advantage. One almost gets the impression that he was reluctant to part with a game that was going so well for him! In other words, he continued with poetry, when it was already time for prose...

Conclusion: The ability to start is not enough without the ability to finish also!

Solution 23

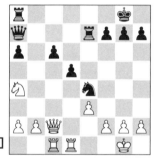

The attentive reader will probably already have noticed that we have the same structure seen in the famous game Flohr-Vidmar (Nottingham 1936). By means of **20.♘c5!** White can place his opponent in a difficult position. Sooner or later Black will have to exchange knights and we will reach a rook endgame similar to that in the aforementioned game, where it is extremely difficult for Black to defend.

However, in the game S.Guliev-Meister (Ceske Budejovice 1993), after long thought, White went in for the sharp line

20.♕xc6

Black replied

20...♘xf2!?

trying to muddy the waters. Strangely, he succeeded:

21.♖d4??

Missing his opponent's reply. By means of 21.♖xd5! or 21.♘b6! White would have retained a favourable position. The following variations demonstrate this:

A) 21.♖xd5 ♘g4 (after 21...♘h3+ 22.♔f1! or 21...♖ae8 22.♕c5 ♕b8 22.♔xf2 White wins) 22.♕b6 ♕xb6 23.♘xb6 ♖ae8 24.♖d3 ♖xe3 25.♖xe3 ♘xe3 26.♔f2 g6 27.♘c4 with material equality; the advanced passed pawn gives White a small plus and Black's position is not easy to defend;

B) 21.♘b6 ♖ae8 22.♔xf2 ♖e6 23.♕c7 ♕xb6 24.♕xb6 ♖xb6 25.♖c2. The computer assesses the position as almost equal, but in the double-rook ending, White's practical chances are somewhat superior.

21...♖xe3!

It may seem strange that, despite thinking for some 40 minutes, White overlooked this simple move. Subconsciously, he thought the e3-pawn was still defended!

22.♕xd5

Black already has serious counterplay, as the following variations demonstrate:

A) 22.♖xd5? ♖e1+ 23.♖xe1 ♘h3+ 24.♔h1 ♕g1+;

B) 22.♔xf2? ♕xd4 23.♕xa8+ ♖e8+;

C) 22.♕b6 ♕e7! 23.♔xf2 ♖e2+ 24.♔f1 ♕e3;

D) Even so, by means of 22.♕c5! ♕xc5 23.♘xc5 (23.♖xc5? ♘d3) 23...♖e2! 24.♔f1! ♖xb2 25.♘a4 ♖xa2 26.♘c3 ♖b2 27.♘a4 White could still maintain equality. This variation was pointed out by the computer.

22...♘d3! 23.♖f1 ♖ae8 24.♘b6 ♖e1 25.♖xd3 ♕xb6+ 26.♕d4 ♖xf1+ 27.♔xf1 ♕e6

Here it is already Black who has the advantage. Unable to cope with such a sudden change of fortune, and in a state of shock, White soon committed a further mistake and even lost.

Conclusion: Never avoid difficulties! Especially when you are playing a serious tournament game, if you wish to win, you must work hard and forget about relaxing.

Especially dangerous is 'automatic play' in superior positions. Not for nothing did Emanuel Lasker say that winning a won position was the hardest thing of all in chess. – Alexander Koblencs

Solution 24

This position is quite complicated. Each side has a territorial advantage

(White on the queenside, Black on the kingside) and would like to break through the opponent's defences on that side. Probably White was hoping to play f3-f4!, strengthening the e5-pawn and restricting the ♗b8, as well as preventing Black's kingside pawn storm. However, it is Black to play and by means of

20...f4!

he breaks through on the kingside, demonstrating that his position is better.

In the game Jirovsky-S.Guliev (Ceske Budejovice 1993), after the moves

21.exf4

(21.gxf4 ♗g6)

21...♗g6! 22.fxg5 ♘xe5 23.♗xe5 ♗xe5 24.♖ae1 ♕xg5 25.♕b3 ♗d4+ 26.♔h1 ♕d2 27.♘f4 ♖xf4!

Black obtained a large advantage. Perhaps a more tenacious defence was 22.♕e2!? (instead of 22.fxg5).

Conclusion: Never miss the moment to attack or seize the initiative!

Only speed has no refutation, except to be faster.

Solution 25

White has an extra pawn, but the control of the second rank, the powerful ♘c3 and the distance of the white queen from the kingside leads us to prefer Black. He stands better.

However, the direct 41...♕f2 42.♖g1 ♘e2 43.♖f1! gives nothing.

Tactics come to his aid!

41...♘e4!

The weakness of the second rank and the scattered white pieces allow this tactical blow. The most tenacious defence is now 42.♖f5! g6! (if 42...♘f2+ 43.♔h2 ♘g4+ 44.♔h1 Black has nothing obvious) 43.♖f3 (43.♖f4 ♘f2+ 44.♔h2 ♘d3!–+) 43...♘f2+ 44.♔h2 ♘g4+ 45.♔h1 ♘xe5 – Black regains the pawn, retaining all of the advantages of his position. But in the game Prandstetter-S.Guliev (Ceske Budejovice 1993) White played weaker:

42.♖xe4?

Also bad are 42.♗xe4 ♕f2, 42.♖g4 ♘f2+ and 42.♖h5 ♕f2–+ (but not 42...♖d3?! 43.♗xe4 ♖xb3 44.♗h7+=).

42...♕c1+! 43.♔h2 ♕f1 44.♖e2 ♕xe2

And Black resigned.

Not for nothing did Nimzowitsch describe the seventh rank as every chess player's first love. Control of this rank often proves decisive for the fate of the game.

Conclusion: Pay attention to the seventh rank!

Will is thought translated into action! – Alexander Bestuzhev-Marlinsky

Solution 26

In the game Jansa-S.Guliev (Ceske Budejovice 1993) Black believed too much in the two bishops and played
21...♗f5?!
but after
22.♗xf6!
(for Black this came like lightning from a clear sky)
22...gxf6 23.g3 ♗d3?!
(23...♖e8!? 24.♘ed4 ♖xe1+ 25.♖xe1 ♗d7=)
24.♘ed4 ♖c4 25.♖e3 ♗c2 26.♘xc2 ♖xc2 27.♖d3
White obtained the better endgame.
  A) Tempting is 21...♘e4!?, but after the moves 22.d3 ♖c2 23.♗e5!, planning to exchange dark-squared bishops and seize the squares c5, d4 and a5 with his knights, White gets a solid advantage;
  B) An interesting try is the pawn sacrifice 21...d4 22.♗xd4 (22.♘exd4 ♗xf4; 22.♘bxd4 ♘d5! 23.g3 ♘b6! with play for both sides) 22...♘d5 23.♗e5 ♗f8!, and the position is unclear. However, it is worth considering 23.g3 (instead of 23.♗e5), and it is not easy for Black to demonstrate that he has sufficient compensation for the pawn;
  C) A reasonable line is 21...♘h5 22.g3 ♖e8! 23.♘bd4 h6 24.♘c3 ♘f6

– the game is roughly equal, but thanks to his two bishops, Black's chances look preferable;
  D) But the strongest was **21...♘e8!** with the intention of transferring the knight to b6, from which it would threaten to come to c4 or a4. In the variation 22.g3 ♘c7 23.♘ed4?! ♘a8! 24.♖ac1 ♘b6 Black's position looks extremely promising.

Conclusion: Routine thinking is a great enemy!

Such is the logic of chess: if you miss your chance, the position can change sharply.
– Alexey Suetin

Solution 27

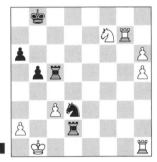

It seems as though it is time for Black to resign, as it is not obvious how the white pawn can be stopped. His only hope is some sort of activity on the queenside.
In the game Timoschenko-S.Guliev (Berlin 1993) Black managed to save the game in unlikely fashion:
43...b4! 44.h7
The most natural. The continuations 44.cxb4? ♖cc2 45.♖g8+ ♔a7 or 44.♘e5 bxc3 45.♘d7+ ♔c8 46.♘xc5? c2+ 47.♔a1 ♖d1+ even lose.
44...bxc3 45.♔a1 ♘b4!

45...c2 46.♖gg1!.

46.h8♕+ ♖c8

An unlikely situation! White has a clear extra queen and in addition it is his move, but it is not clear how he can win. During the game, after long thought, White chose the following continuation, which led to an equal endgame:

47.♖g2 ♖xg2 48.♕e5+ ♖c7
The only move.
49.♕e8+ ♔a7 50.♕e3+ ♔b8
51.♕e8+ ♔a7 52.♕e3+ ♔b8
53.♕e6 ♖xa2+ 54.♕xa2 ♘xa2
55.♔xa2

55.h6? ♖xf7 56.h7 ♖xh7 57.♖xh7 c2, and Black even wins.

55...♖xf7 56.♔b3 ♔c7 57.♔xc3 ♔d6 58.♔d4 ♔e6

And the players agreed a draw. One of your authors, who played Black in this game, returned to the diagram position many times subsequently and it seemed to him that the game had ended with the rightful result. But the path to the truth is not always a straight one! When working as trainer of the Turkish team, he (the author) showed the position to his assistant, IM G.Killizhaslan. The latter, looking at the position with fresh eyes, suggested the move 44.♖g5! (instead of 44.h7). As the following

variations show, White does win after all:

A) 44...b3 45.axb3! (45.♖xc5 ♖b2+ 46.♔a1 ♖xa2+ 47.♔b1 ♖b2+=) 45...♖xc3 46.♖a5+−;

B) 44...♖xg5 45.h7! (45.♘xg5 bxc3−+) 45...bxc3 46.h8♕+;

C) Nor can Black save himself with 44...♖c4 45.h7 bxc3 46.h8♕+ ♔a7 47.♔a1! c2 48.♖gg1+−.

So, we can say that the position is winning for White! As well as that, White actually has at his disposal a second way to win. In the variation which occurred in the game, he can play more precisely. Specifically: 45.h8♕+ (instead of 45.♔a1) 45...♖c8 46.♕xc8+ ♔xc8 47.♘d6+ ♔d8 48.♖g8+ ♔d7 49.♖c8! and now, for example: 49...♘f2 50.h6 ♖b2+ 51.♔a1 ♘xh1 52.h7 ♖f2 53.♔b1 ♖b2+ 54.♔c1.

Conclusion: Resignation is always too early!

There are always more people in the world who resign than are actually lost.

Solution 28

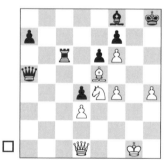

If he wishes, White can give perpetual check at once (41.♕h5+ ♔g8 42.♕g4+). But the bad position of the enemy king and White's excellently-coordinated forces tempt him to play for more. This temptation is extremely hard to resist and he did not manage to do so in the game Gadzhili-S.Guliev (Nikolaev 1993). With

41.♘g5!?

he decided to play for a win. There followed:

41...♗h6! 42.♘xf7+ ♔h7 43.♘g5+

The open position of the white king ties his hands and he cannot give up the attack.

43...♗xg5! 44.hxg5

Here White could still force a draw with 44.♕h5+ ♗h6 45.♕f7+ ♔h8 46.♕e8+.

44...♔g6!

It is easy to see that all of Black's moves are forced.

45.f7

45...♕a3!

As Gadzhili himself admitted after the game, he had missed this move in his original calculations. Suddenly Black obtains counterplay.

46.♔h2 ♔xf7!?

It was worth considering 46...♖c8!? with the idea of ...♖c8-f8-f7.

47.♗f6?!

But now Black starts to dictate events. After 47.♕h5+ ♔e7 48.♕h7+ ♔d8 49.♗xd4 ♕c1 the game remains unclear.

47...♔g8! 48.♗xd4 a5 49.♕h5?

This is the decisive mistake; it was essential to play 49.♔g3 and the position remains sharp.

49...♖c2+ 50.♔h1 ♕c1+ 51.♗g1 ♕xf4 52.g6

He also loses after both 52.♕g6+ ♔f8 53.♕h6+ ♔e7 and 52.♕e8+ ♔g7 53.♕e7+ ♔g6 54.♕xe6+ ♔h5!, and the black king escapes from the checks.

52...♖c7 53.♕h3 ♕f5 54.♕g3 e5 55.d4 ♕e4+ 56.♔h2 ♖c2+ 0-1

Although the game ended in a black win after a bitter struggle, for a long time the position was balanced. If, over the board, you can control yourself and do not give way to temptation, but calmly calculate the variations, then this means you have nerves of steel! But if you are not sufficiently calm, then you need to work on this. As the great Tamburlaine said:

The ability to stop in time is a quality essential for war!

Conclusion: In all circumstances, it is essential to remain calm.

Solution 29

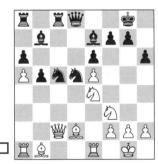

The first thought which comes into one's head when one looks at the position is: can we exploit White's domination of the diagonal b1-h7? The attentive reader will not be deceived: White is (slightly) better!

A) 20.♘d6! ♗xd6 21.♕h7+ ♔f8 22.exd6 ♕xd6 23.♘e5;

B) Not good is 20.♘eg5 because of 20...f5! and Black is better (20...♗xg5 (20...hxg5 21.♕h7+ ♔f8 22.♕h8#; 20...g6 21.♘xf7) 21.♕h7+ ♔f8 22.♘xg5 ♘c3!∓ (22...hxg5 23.♕h8+ ♔e7 24.♗xg5+ f6 25.♕xg7+ ♔e8 26.♗g6#; 22...♘e7 23.♕h8+ ♘g8 24.♗h7+−)).

In the game S.Guliev-Savchenko (Nikolaev 1993) White's head began to spin from all the tempting possibilities, and he chose one of the weakest moves and even managed to lose.

20.♘xc5?! ♗xc5 21.♕h7+ ♔f8 22.♕h8+?!

22.♘g5 or 22.♗e4 allows White to retain a sufficient initiative.

22...♔e7 23.♕xg7

23...♕h8!

This is the move White missed in his initial calculations! He had been counting on 23...♕g8 24.♕xh6 with a large advantage. Here we again can see how important it is to control the board throughout the entire game.

24.♕g4

Since the black king lacks secure cover, White wanted to keep the queens on the board. This idea is fatal, because the white king is even more vulnerable!

24...♖g8! 25.♕h4+ ♔d7

It is easy to see that Black is ruler of the position. But even so, there was no need to make the following move, which loses immediately.

26.♗xh6?? ♗e7! 27.♕h5 ♖xg2+! 28.♔f1

28.♔xg2 ♘f4+.

28...♖ag8 29.♗e4 ♖2g6 0-1

After the game, the white player was in shock. It was as clear as day to him after the game that he needed to work on playing standard positions. This was especially true of organising an attack on a king which is inadequately protected.

Conclusion: Standard methods of attacking a king must be known!

He who takes a risk might lose, but he who does not take a risk definitely loses!
– Savielly Tartakower

Solution 30

The position is equal. White only needs not to allow ...e5-e4, cutting off his light-squared bishop from his king, after which Black could obtain a strong attack. Thus, the answer to the question 'is the move 37.♗f3 possible?' is that it is essential!

In the game Nevednichy-S.Guliev (Nikolaev 1993) White thereby constructed an unbreachable fortress:

37.♗f3!

He cannot delay. After 37.♗d5+ ♔g6 38.♗f3 ♔h5! 39.♗xg4+ ♔xg4 followed by ...e5-e4 and ...♗e5 Black gets good winning chances.

37...e4

Nor does anything come from 37...♔e6 38.♗xg4 fxg4 39.♔f1! ♔d5 40.♔e2 ♔e4 41.♗a5.

38.♗xg4 fxg4 39.♔f1 ♔e6 40.♔e2 ♔d5 41.♗e1 ♔c4 42.♗a5 ♗a7 43.♗c7 ♗c5 44.♗a5 ♔d4 45.♗d2 ♗d6 46.♗e3+ ♔c4 47.♗f2 ♗b4 48.♔e3 ♗c5+ ½-½

In his textbook, Capablanca advised that one strive for exchanges when material ahead. Our example shows that sometimes exchanges favour the weaker side!

Conclusion: Exceptions to the general rule are common in the endgame!

The laws of chess fall down on the fact that the weaker side needs sometimes to exchange pieces, as, after all, a lone bishop or even two knights cannot force checkmate against a bare king. The defender needs to aim for a typical position where his chances of a draw increase, such as opposite-coloured bishops, a rook ending, a possible fortress, etc. – Alexander Panchenko

Solution 31

An interesting position. At first glance, Black is in a bad way. The ♗b7 and pawn on c6 give White a large space advantage. However, tactics come to Black's aid. The position is equal.

In the game Neverov-S.Guliev (Nikolaev 1993) Black seized the initiative with the help of an exchange sacrifice:

32...♖bxb7!

And after

33.cxb7 ♖xb7 34.♖cd1? ♖c7! 35.♖c1 ♖d7 36.♖ed1 a5 37.♘c6 ♗xa3! 38.♖a1 ♗b4 39.♘xa5 ♗g4 40.♘c6 ♗xd1

the advantage was already on his side.

White should not have forced the position! The calm 34.♖ed1!? would have assured him equality.

Dear reader, be careful with two bishops! As Nimzowitsch said long ago:

Two bishops are a fearsome weapon in capable hands.

Conclusion: Every chess player should be able to handle the two bishops well.

85

Solution 32

The white pieces are excellently mobilised, but at the same time, his pawn structure, especially on the kingside, is significantly weakened. Which of these two factors will prove the more important will determine the assessment of the position.

In the game Fogarasi-S.Guliev (Ostrava 1993), White, with the intention of extracting the benefits from his active pieces, played the resolute

20.f5!?

There followed

20...♘c5 21.♕c3 ♘a4 22.♕b3 ♕xb3 23.axb3 ♖xd4! 24.fxe6 ♖h4+ 25.♔g1 ♗c5+ 26.♗e3 fxe6

and thanks to the enemy pawn weaknesses Black obtained the advantage. Black's position is better. Perhaps White should have chosen 20.♘e5, settling for passive defence, although even then, after 20...♕xd3 21.♘xd3 ♘b6 Black's game should be preferred. The weaknesses on d4, f4 and h5 are obvious. Philidor was right:

Pawns are the soul of the game.

Conclusion: Advancing pawns promises gains in space, but at the same time weakens one's base. One must always ask oneself which is more important in each concrete case.

Solution 33

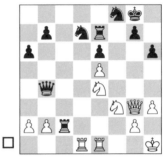

It appears that Black has nothing to fear. There are no direct threats, and he is extremely active on the queenside. However, the reader's penetrating gaze has probably spotted that the black pieces lack coordination.

In the encounter S.Guliev-Michenka (Ostrava 1993) White, looking at Black's piece configuration, immediately recalled the famous game Marshall-Rubinstein (Moscow 1925). This helped him to find his next move:

34.♕h4!

Threatening both 35.♘f6+ and 35.a3. There followed

34...♔h8 35.a3 ♘g6 36.axb4 ♘xh4 37.♘xh4

and White soon won.

Black could have tried 34...♖xb2, although after 35.♖d4 ♕a3 36.♘d6! (36.♖a4 ♕xa4 37.♘f6+ ♘xf6 38.♕xa4 ♘d5=) 36...♘g6 37.♕e4 ♘gf8 38.♘c4 White is better.

Conclusion: Sometimes the queen can usefully remember its right to move just one square at a time!

One cannot become a real chess player without a serious study of the classics, just as one cannot, for example, imagine a great writer or painter who has not read Shakespeare or examined the paintings of Rembrandt. – Mark Dvoretsky, Artur Jussupow

Solution 34

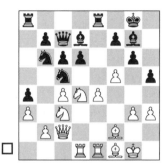

We have a middlegame characteristic of the main line of the g3-King's Indian Defence. Careful examination reveals that White has made serious progress on the kingside. In addition, with his last move ...h7-h5 Black has seriously weakened the g6-square. Exploiting this nuance, White obtains a serious advantage. The game S.Guliev-Novotny (Pardubice 1993) continued:
25.fxg6 fxg6 26.e5!
By exploiting the weakened position of the black king, White goes over to active operations.
26...dxe5 27.♕xg6 exd4 28.♗xd4 ♘e6 29.♗e5 ♕d8 30.♗d3 ♕g5 31.♕h7+ ♔f7 32.♗g6+! ♔e7
32...♕xg6 33.♖f1+.
33.♗d6+ ♔d8 34.♗xe8 ♗d4+ 35.♖xd4 ♘xd4 36.♗e7+
And Black resigned.

Conclusion: In regularly playing this or that opening variation, one should carefully study each side's typical plans and technical devices.

The advance of pawns should not take one outside the realm of safety. – Georgy Lisitsin

Solution 35

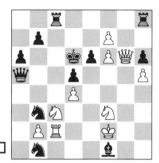

Black has a huge material advantage, but his king is in a critical position. White managed to exploit this circumstance in the game Zvara-S.Guliev (Pardubice 1993), and ended the game at once with a tactic. White is winning.
29.♘b5+!
After this move, Black can only resign. As shown by the variation 29...♗xb5 30.♕g3+ ♔d7 31.♘e5+ ♔d6 (31...♔d8 32.♕g8+) 32.♘c4+, he has no choice. Black momentarily forgot that the most important piece in a chess game is the king, and its safety outstrips everything. He paid the price for this.

Conclusion: Never forget about king safety!

The decisive role (in work) is played not always by material, but by the master. – Maxim Gorky

Solution 36

Black's pawn on h6 is hanging and the assessment of the position depends on how successfully he can meet this threat. It appears that he has to play 25...g5, but this gives White the advantage. However, Black has an unusual way to obtain the superior game.

In the game Chuchelov-L.Guliev (Dresden 1994) there followed the unexpected (for White)

25...♗g5!

and it became clear which side had the initiative. Evidently, White should have settled for 26.♖g3, after which Black is clearly better, but nothing decisive is apparent. However, at the board, White decided to accept the pawn:

26.♘xg5?!

Also after 26.♗xg5 hxg5 27.♖xh8 ♕xh8 28.♘xg5 ♕h4 29.f3 ♖h8 Black's game should be preferred.

26...hxg5 27.♗xg5

Nor is 27.♖xh8 ♕xh8 28.♗xg5 ♕h3 any better.

27...♕xg5!!

In all probability, White had overlooked this queen sacrifice. However, if this possibility were not available, Black would simply stand badly!

28.♕xg5 ♖xh3

For the queen, Black has obtained 'Laskerian compensation' (admittedly, Lasker usually sacrificed the queen for rook, knight and pawn, whereas here Black is even a pawn down!). Now the excellently-organised black forces storm the white bastions. The rooks seize the h-file, whilst the knights enter the enemy camp via the weak squares. White's scattered forces can put up no resistance.

29.♕d2 ♖ah8 30.g5 ♘d3!

Black does not hurry to take the h2-pawn – it is not going anywhere and first it is necessary to include the knights in the attack.

31.♔g1 ♘7c5 32.f3 ♘xb4 33.axb4 ♘b3 34.♕a2 ♘d4 35.♕xa6 ♖xh2 36.♘d1 ♖h1+ 37.♔f2 ♖8h2+

And White resigned.

In several games, the ex-World Champion Emanuel Lasker sacrificed his queen for rook, knight and pawn, obtaining in return good counterplay and then instructively demonstrating the pieces' superiority over the queen! Therefore this material balance is known in chess literature as 'Lasker compensation'. By way of an example, there is the game Euwe-Lasker, Zurich 1934. However, this is by no means Lasker's only discovery, as is emphasised by the well-known quote:

Numerous ideas in chess art are unthinkable without Lasker. – Alexander Alekhine

Conclusion: Do not be mean with the queen!

Solution 37

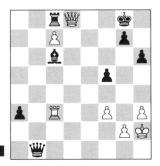

Here you can train your calculation of variations, as well as testing your knowledge of standard positions in queen endgames. The position is equal. The correct reply is **37...♔h7!!**
38.♕xc8 a2:

A) 39.♖c1 ♗b7! (39...a1♕? 40.♖xb1 ♕xb1 41.♕b8+−) 40.♖xb1 axb1♕ 41.♕b8 ♕a1 (41...♕e1=) 42.♕xb7 ♕e5+=;

B) 39.♖a3 ♗b7 40.♕b8 a1♕ 41.♖xa1 ♕xa1 42.♕xb7 ♕e5+ and Black gives perpetual check. As we see, in this way Black can draw the game.
In the game Kortchnoi-S.Guliev (Moscow 1994) Black calculated variations for a long time and decided that there was not a great difference between the moves 37...♖xd8 and 37...♔h7. There followed:
37...♖xd8??

38.cxd8♕+ ♔h7
Now White could have won by means of 39.♖xa3!! (this move Black had overlooked) 39...♕b4 40.♖d3! ♕f4+ 41.♔g1 ♕c1+ 42.♖d1 etc. However, in time trouble, he played
39.♖xc6?!
and after
39...a2

40.♕d6?
finally missed the win.
But he could still have achieved the latter: 40.♖c8! a1♕ 41.♕g8+ ♔g6 42.♖c6+ ♕f6 43.♕e8+ ♔g5 44.h4+! ♔xh4 45.♖xf6 (45.g3+! ♔g5 46.f4+ ♔g4 47.♕e2#) 45...gxf6 46.♕g6 – this variation was pointed out the next day by Kortchnoi himself. Did you find it, dear reader?
Now, however, play leads by force to a queen ending, where White has three pawns versus two on the same side. Despite the extra pawn, theory considers the position drawn.
40...f4 41.♖a6 a1♕ 42.♖xa1 ♕xa1 43.♕xf4
And despite lengthy attempts by White to realise his extra pawn, the game ended in a draw.

Akiba Rubinstein wrote:

When you have a choice, the possibility of a mistake increases.

Conclusion: Sometimes the king should move unexpectedly!

Solution 38

White has a strong passed pawn on a5 and in order to blockade it, Black has to maintain his knight in a passive position. However, his other forces are actively placed and the majority are pointing at the white king, whose position is seriously weakened. The position is equal.
In the encounter Paronian-S.Guliev (Kstovo 1994) Black managed to organise a strong attack:
21...♘f4! 22.♖ad1
22.♘g5! ♘e6 23.♘xe6 ♖xe6 24.♕xb5 ♖h6 25.♗c1 ♖h5=.
22...♕h3 23.♘e3 ♘c5!
The most passive black piece jumps into the game with tempo, deciding the game.
24.♕xb5 ♕h5 25.♘h2
Or 25.gxf4 ♕xf3 and then ...♖e8-e6-g6.
25...♘h3+ 26.♔g2 ♘xf2 27.♖d2 ♖b8 28.♕c6 ♘cxd3 0-1

Conclusion: If one piece stands badly, the whole game is not always bad!

... the air around the enemy king is also of great significance. – Bent Larsen

Solution 39

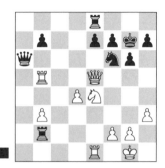

The defence involves a non-standard rook manoeuvre.
25...♖c2! 26.g4 h6
27.h4 ♖c6! 28.g5 hxg5 29.hxg5 ♖e6! 30.gxf6+ exf6! and Black has the advantage.
In the game Uhlmann-L.Guliev (Dresden 1994), White, anticipating his opponent's idea, turned aside earlier:
27.♘xf6
And after
27...♕xf6 28.♕xf6+ ♔xf6 29.♖xb7 ♖d2!
a double rook ending was reached, where despite White's extra pawn, Black's active pieces give him good drawing chances.
30.♖e4 g5 31.b4 e6 32.b5 ♖d8 33.b6 ♖8xd4 34.♖xd4 ♖xd4 35.♖c7 ♖b4 36.b7 ♔g6 37.♔f1 ♖b2 38.♔e1 f5 39.♔d1 ♔f6 40.♔c1 ♖b6 41.♔d2 ♔e5 42.♖d7 fxg4 43.hxg4 ♔f4 44.♔c3 e5 45.♔d3 ♔xg4 46.♔e4 ♖b5 47.♖h7 h5 ½-½

A variation occurs on the board when its assessment satisfies both players. This happens when both like the subjective evaluation or one of them misjudges the position, over- or underestimating its individual factors, or, finally, when the assessment is complicated and involves

many factors for each side. – Peter Romanovsky

It should be added that the manoeuvre on which Black's defence is based reminds one very much of that used in the game Pirc-Capablanca (Moscow 1936).

Conclusion: When it comes to divining the opponent's intentions, better late than never!

Solution 40

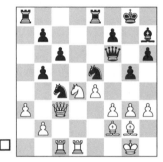

The position is quite complicated, but is equal. White has two bishops but his pawn mass is well blockaded. The main question is whether White will manage to play f3-f4 or whether Black will prevent it and force the opponent into passive defence.
In the game Dyachkov-S.Guliev (Minsk 1994) White, considering that he stood better, decided on active operations, opening the d-file and attacking the weak dark squares on the queenside. With this intention, he played
23.♘b3?
but after
23...♘xb2! 24.♖f1
(24.♕xb2 ♘xf3+)
24...♘bd3 25.f4 ♘xc1 26.♖xc1 ♘d7

Black obtained a winning position.
A) Somewhat better was 23.♘e2!? (with the intention of f3-f4) 23...♘xb2 24.f4 ♘xd1 25.♖xd1 gxf4 26.gxf4 ♕g7!, and we reach a position which is difficult to assess and with mutual chances;
B) An even stronger-looking move is 23.b3: 23...♘xa3 23.♕e3 ♕e7 24.f4 ±; or
C) 23.♕c2 – in this way, White maintains approximate equality;
D) Not good is 23.♔h2 (intending to continue ♗g1, ♖f1 and f3-f4) because of 23...♗xe4.

Conclusion: Never forget about x-ray attacks!

Never miss a single chance to solve combinative puzzles. – Alexander Kotov

Solution 41

White's advantage is obvious. The g7-pawn and the poor position of the black king allow White to win with a long combination. White is winning. The game S.Guliev-Alavkin (Minsk 1994) ended as follows:
19.♖xa8+ ♗xa8 20.♕a1! ♕b8
20...♗b7 21.♕a7!; 20...♔d7 21.♕a7+ ♕c7 22.♕xc7+ ♔xc7 23.♖h8 ♖xg7 24.♖xa8.

21.♖h8 ♔e7 22.♘e4 e5 23.♖xg8 ♕xg8 24.♕a7+ ♔e6 25.♕d7+!
And in view of the variation
25...♔xd7 26.♘f6+ and ♘xg8 Black resigned.

Conclusion: A passed pawn is a great strength!

A far advanced passed pawn is virtually the basis of a combination. – Peter Romanovsky

Solution 42

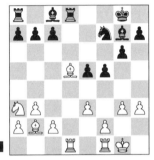

On account of the greater activity of his pieces, White's position is undoubtedly better. Black faces a difficult choice – the threat is 16.♗xf7+. How can he parry this threat?
In the game S.Guliev-Rustemov (Minsk 1994) Black played
15...♖d7?
and after the moves
16.♗xb7! ♖xd1 17.♗xa8 ♖d8 18.♗g2
remained a pawn down.
A) 15...♖e8? also fails to solve the problem because of 16.♘b5! ♖e7 17.♗a3;
B) Only **15...♖f8!** permits Black to retain material equality and stay in the game. For example: 16.♘b5 c6 17.♘c7 ♖b8 18.♗e6 b6! 19.♗xc8

(19.♗a3! c5 20.♗d5±) 19...♖fxc8! 20.♘a6 ♖b7=.
As this variation shows, White's initiative can gradually be extinguished, because he has nothing concrete.

Conclusion: Never forget about the chance of a discovered attack.

A discovered attack without check is harder to anticipate. This element especially enters complicated combinations. – Georgy Lisitsin

Solution 43

On the board we have a complicated and dynamic position. White has sacrificed a pawn and kept the black king in the centre, where it can come under attack. But this is not so easy to organise, e.g. 21.♘b3 ♕d6 22.♖fd1 ♕b6! and White has nothing.
In the game Panchenko-S.Guliev (Minsk 1994) White decided to continue the attack by means of
21.♘f5!
and after
21...exf5 22.♖fe1+ ♖e7 23.♗c6+ ♗xc6 24.♕xc6+ ♕d7
(24...♘d7? 25.♖xe7+ ♕xe7 26.♕c8+ ♕d8 27.♖e1+−)
25.♖xe7+ ♔xe7 26.♕c5+ ♕d6

(26...♔e8? 27.♖b1!)
27.♖e1+ ♔d7
(27...♘e4? 28.♕xf5)
28.♕a7+ ♔d8 29.♕a8+ ♔d7
30.♕b7+ ♔d8 31.♕a8+
the players agreed a draw.
One of Capablanca's principles was:

Attack the enemy king energetically with all available resources, in order to ensure success. Once started, the attack must be carried through to the end.

As you see, in this game, the experienced grandmaster Alexander Nikolaevich Panchenko followed his advice!

Conclusion: The attack develops from the outward picture of the position.

Solution 44

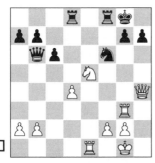

White has an isolated pawn. At the same time, his pieces are very active and are unequivocally pointing at the enemy king. An attentive study of the position leads to the conclusion that White has a chance for a beautiful combination! If you have good tactical vision and can calculate variations well, then you will be in no doubt: White is winning.

In the game S.Guliev-Kobalia (Moscow 1994) there followed:
34.♖xg7+! ♔xg7 35.♕g5+ ♔h8
36.♘g6+! ♔g8
Or 36...hxg6 37.♕h6+ ♔g8
38.♕xg6+ ♔h8 39.♖e7.

Unfortunately, at this point, the abundance of winning continuations caused White's eyes to glaze over and, as often happens in such situations, he started to err.
37.♖e7?!
Both 37.♘xf8+ and 37.♘f4+ lead to a win, but the most aesthetic continuation was 37.♘h8+! (the erudite reader will undoubtedly recall the famous game Kotov-Keres, Budapest Candidates 1950) 37...♔xh8 38.♖e7 ♘h5 39.♕h6.
37...♘e4! 38.♕e5?
It was not too late to win with 38.♕g4.
38...♖f6 39.♕h5 ♖f7 40.♖xf7
♔xf7 41.♘e5+ ♔g7 42.♕g4+
♔f6 43.♕f4+ ♔g7 44.♕g4+ ♔f6
45.♕f4+ ♔g7 ½-½
What to do – such collapses happen to every player...

History is the best teacher but has the worst pupils. – Indira Ghandi

Conclusion: The corner squares are also part of the chessboard! Don't forget about them.

Solution 45

By way of compensation for his ruined queenside pawn structure, Black has actively-placed pieces. This factor is the more important, and so Black stands better. In such positions, where a temporary advantage (better developed pieces) offsets a permanent one (weak pawn structure), the value of every move is especially high! Frequently, every move is potentially decisive in determining the outcome of the game.

In the game S.Guliev-Ljubojevic (Moscow 1994) the master of dynamic play that is Ljubojevic quickly showed that in this position, development is the more important factor!

13...♕xd4! 14.♕xd4 ♖xd4 15.♗e3 c5! Black's whole combinative idea hangs on this move!

16.♗xd4 cxd4 17.♘b5 d3! 18.♖ec1? Now Black obtains the advantage. More tenacious was 18.♘c3!?, with a complicated game ahead.

18...♘xe4 19.♖xc4 ♘d2! 20.♖c5 ♗xg2 21.♔xg2 ♘e4 22.♖c4 f5! 23.a4 a6 24.♘c3 ♘d6 25.♖c7 ♖xb2 And Black's superiority assumed real dimensions.

At the board, the idea of an exchange sacrifice did not enter

White's head until Black played 15... c5!.

Conclusion: First impressions can often be deceptive.

Ideas can only be neutralised by ideas. – Honoré de Balzac

Solution 46

It is generally accepted that in the endgame, three pawns are usually stronger than a piece. However, here the white king is very active. Based on this, White decided that he stood better and sought victory in various long variations. However, in the game S.Guliev-Balashov (St Petersburg 1994) the grandmaster refuted his opponent's expectations with a few accurate moves. White was given a lesson in top-class endgame technique. The position is equal.

58...f6!

A) But not 58...f5 59.♔f4 g6 60.♔e5+–; or

B) 58...g5? 59.♔e4!;

C) But it was worth considering 58...h5!?.

Here we again see the workings of 'Capablanca's rule', which points out how one should place one's pawns – they should be arranged so as to limit the enemy bishop's scope (see example 119 on this theme).

59.♔g4

In the event of 59.♔e4 ♔f7 60.♔d5 h5 61.♔c6?! (61.♔e4!) 61...h4 62.♔b6 h3 63.♗c7 g5 64.♔xa6 f5! 65.♗h2 f4 66.♔xb5 f3 67.♗g3 f2 Black even wins.

59...♔f7! 60.♔h5 ♔e6!= 61.♔g6 ♔d5 62.♔xg7 h5 63.♗xf6 a5!!

This is what reveals Black's main idea. Exploiting the fact that the a8-square is inaccessible to the white bishop, he takes play into a theoretically drawn endgame. Admittedly, White has two extra pawns on the a-file, but in this case, it is of no significance.

64.bxa5 ♔c6 65.♔f7 ♔b7

And the players soon agreed a draw. White cannot create a zugzwang to exploit the presence of the b5-pawn.

Conclusion: How many forms of fortress do you know of in bishop endings?

The king can defend himself. –
Wilhelm Steinitz

Solution 47

Because the white rook and bishop on the queenside have no moves, Black has a large advantage.

However, as a first thing, he should free himself from the pin on the h4-d8 diagonal. But after 21...g5 22.♗g3 White gets good prospects on the kingside. He has the threats of d3-d4, h3-h4, ♘d5 or ♘f5 etc. In view of this, in the game Sabyanov-L.Guliev (Kstovo 1994) Black decided to exploit the hidden resources of the position and sacrificed the queen for two minor pieces.

21...♘e8!! 22.♘d5 ♗xh4 23.♘xc7 ♘xc7

Suddenly it turns out that, despite his large material advantage, White's position is hopeless, because it is not obvious how the imprisoned pieces can be brought into the game. When the opponent has a bad piece (or pieces), it is necessary to try to exchange his active ones. Sometimes, in order to do this, one needs not just to exchange pieces of equal value, but even sacrifice material. In chess literature, this is called a positional sacrifice.

24.♕d1 ♘e6 25.♖e3 ♗g5 26.♕f3

White does not know what to do.

If there are no good moves, one ends up playing bad ones! This is an old truth. –
Siegbert Tarrasch

26...♔g7
It seems that this refusal to take the exchange wins most quickly of all. Black regroups his forces, aiming at the enemy king. Although nominally ahead, White is helpless: the black pieces are so active that White has no chances of saving the game.
27.♕g3 ♗f4 28.♕g2 ♖h8 29.h4 h5 30.g5 ♖hf8 31.♖e1 f6 32.gxf6+ ♖xf6 33.♖d1 ♖df8 34.d4 c4 35.dxe5 ♗xe5 36.♖d5 ♖f4 37.♖a5 ♗c8 38.♖xa4 ♖g4 0-1

Conclusion: Material does not always triumph.

Aces do not win in every game! –
Kozma Prutkov

Solution 48

The correct assessment is that White is winning. As the reader has probably already guessed, the position is a *tabiya* from the Dragon Sicilian. Black often plays the manoeuvre ...♖a8-c8-c5, preparing the move ...b7-b5, so as to start serious counterplay on the queenside.
In the game L.Guliev-Fedorov (Kstovo 1994) the well-known Belorussian GM, a noted Dragon specialist, had played a novelty. He

decided to sacrifice the b-pawn and then play ...♖a8-c8-c5 with tempo and obtain a serious initiative. Thus, we reached the position in the diagram. However, he had missed a small nuance.

Small mistakes lead to bigger ones. –
Lucius Annaeus Seneca

These words are very apt here!
15.♘xd6!
The white pieces in the centre occupy dominating positions, whilst the black pieces, by contrast, are hanging. These factors make the sacrifice possible.
15...exd6 16.♕xd6 ♕c8 17.♗xf6 ♖c6 18.♕xe5 ♗xf6 19.♕f4 ♗xc3 20.bxc3 ♗e6 21.♔b2 ♖xc3 22.♖d2
And White has two extra pawns for no compensation.

Conclusion: When changing the move-order in well-known opening positions, be careful!

Negligence in small things can cause big problems. – Benjamin Franklin

Solution 49

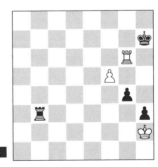

Thanks to the strong position of his rook, which cuts off the black king, White should draw.

The game Remizov-S.Guliev (St Petersburg 1994) confirmed this assessment.

68...♖b2+ 69.♔g1

Mistaken is 69.♔g3 ♖g2+, but 69.♔h1 does not lose either.

69...♖g2+ 70.♔h1

Black is in zugzwang.

70...g3

Nothing is given by 70...♖g3 71.♔h2 or 70...♔h8 71.f6!. Now, however, the black rook loses a square for manoeuvring, which allows White to direct the game to a draw.

71.♖g4 ♔h6 72.♖h4+ ♔g5 73.♖xh3 ♖h2+ ½-½

It is claimed that Archimedes once said:

Give me a strong enough base and I could support the whole world.

In our example, the white rook obtains such support in the form of the f5-pawn. Tarrasch famously said that in rook endings, the best post for the rook is behind the passed pawn, be it an enemy pawn or one's own. In our example, following these two classical principles (the rook initially stood behind the black pawns and then switched behind its own) saved the game.

Conclusion: *All rook endings are drawn. – Tarrasch*

Solution 50

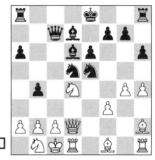

The splendid centralisation of the black pieces is, unfortunately, deceptive and it would be quite wrong to assess the position solely on that basis! A deeper examination reveals the hidden weaknesses of the black position. His king is still in the centre and his major pieces, especially his rooks, are not yet in the game. And although his minor pieces occupy active positions, these posts cannot be described as secure. As a result, White has a large advantage.

Black does not need more than 2-3 moves (...0-0, ...♖fd8 etc.) and already White will have problems. This means that the advantage is a temporary one and White needs to act quickly.

In the game L.Guliev-Galliamova (Kstovo 1994) there followed

17.♘f5! ♗c5 18.♕e2

and Black fell under a fearsome attack, which can hardly be repulsed.

18...f6 19.f4 ♘xg4 20.♖xd5 ♘xh2 21.♘xg7+ ♔f8 22.♖xd7 ♕xd7 23.♘xe6+ ♔f7 24.♘xc5 ♕d4 25.♕c4+ ♕xc4 26.♗xc4+ 1-0

Conclusion: Appearances are deceptive!

For Black, the Sicilian presents a crisis – if you take a risk, you might get mated, but if you don't, the best you can hope for is an endgame a pawn down. Better to take the risk! – Leonid Stein

Solution 51

White has two extra pawns. Black needs to do something quickly, else he will just lose. Surprising as it may seem, the activity of the black pieces is fully adequate to hold the balance. The position is drawn. The game Semeniuk-S.Guliev (Vladivostok 1994) ended as follows:
32...♗xg2! 33.♔xg2 ♖g6+ 34.♔h1 ♕f3+ 35.♔h2 ♕f4+ ½-½
More interesting is 33.♕xg2, but after 33...♖g6 34.♖d4 ♖xg2+ 35.♔xg2 ♕g5+ 36.♖g4 ♕f6 Black has sufficient counterplay, on account of the weak position of the white king. When one player has a static advantage (better pawn structure, two bishops, extra material, etc.), whilst the other has a dynamic advantage (e.g. a lead in development), then factors such as time, the calculation of variations and combinative imagination come to the fore.

Conclusion: Desperation is also an act.

In some positions, waiting tactics may prolong the game, but won't save it. – Rudolf Spielmann

Solution 52

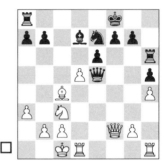

The game L.Guliev-Skomorokhin (Kstovo 1994) continued:
19.dxe6 ♗xe6 20.♖he1 ♕f5 21.♕xa7!

This move is the point of White's combination.
21...♕f4+ 22.♔b1 ♕b8 23.♕c5 ♕c8 24.♕xc8+ ♖xc8 25.♗xe6 ♖xe6 26.♖xe6 fxe6 27.♖d7
And White soon won.

Conclusion: Everything for the sake of victory!

In some positions a combination is as natural as a baby's smile. – Reuben Fine

Solution 53

The position is extremely sharp
and complicated. On the queenside,
power lies exclusively in White's
hands, but Black has superior force
on the kingside. In such positions,
a chess player is helped by such
qualities as tactical imagination,
the ability to calculate variations
well and a knowledge of standard
technical devices.

At first glance, White has a large
advantage, because it is hard to
believe that Black's minimal
forces will be able to create serious
threats against the enemy king.
Surprisingly, though, they can!
The position is equal. If White is
greedy and plays 38.♖xc6? then he
falls into an instructive trap: 38...g3!
39.hxg3 ♖f2!! 40.♔xf2 h2 and Black
wins.

As Napoleon said:

*Any commander can win by using his
own forces, a real commander is the
one who can win by utilising the enemy
forces.*

In the above variation, the black
pawn on h2 utilises the white
pawns on g2 and c5 to prevent the
white king or rook from stopping
its promotion.

In the game Kharitonov-S.Guliev
(Moscow 1995) White, despite
serious time trouble, spotted this
neat trap and played:
38.♖b7
After
38...♖f5 39.♖b1 ♖f7
(also possible is 39...hxg2 40.♔xg2
♘f3!)
**40.♖f1 ♖b7 41.♖f4 g3 42.hxg3 ♖b2
43.♖f2 ♖a2 44.♘f3 ♖a1+ 45.♔h2
hxg2 46.♔xg2 ♘e4 47.♖b2 ♖xa4
48.♘e5 ♖b4 49.♖a2 a4 50.♘xc6 ♖b3
51.♖xa4**
the opponents agreed a draw.
38.♖b1 also leads to equality.

Conclusion: Chess is inexhaustible.
One must always be on the alert!

*Time is space for developing one's
abilities. – Karl Marx*

Solution 54

White has a very strong outpost
on the d-file. However, he has
insufficient resources to support
the advanced piece. His forces are
scattered and his pawn structure
weakened. Soon we will see that
White does not have that much
time to regain the e3-pawn. Black is
winning.

In the game Golod-S.Guliev (Agios Nikolaos 1995) Black demonstrated this in the following manner:
23...a5!
Opening lines for his rooks, with the aim of attacking White's weaknesses.
Nimzowitsch wrote long ago that

If a weakness cannot be attacked, then it does not matter.

White's camp contains numerous weaknesses, but for the moment, the black forces cannot attack them. But soon Black will organise such an attack and then we will see their vulnerability!
24.♖b1
24.a3 axb4 25.axb4 ♖a8.
24...axb4 25.♖xb4 ♖a8 26.a4 ♖a5 27.♖c4 ♖fa8 28.♖dd4 ♖8a6 29.♗f1 b5! 30.cxb6 ♖xb6−+

Black's large advantage is already beyond dispute and he soon won. In military science, great importance is attached to communications between the front and the rear. Such lines of communication, like blood vessels in the body, are essential for the carrying out of any operation. In our example, it is clear that this is so in chess as well!

Conclusion: It is useful to have a 'reserve' open file!

Be careful not to advance too far! – Virgil

Solution 55

White has two bishops in active positions. His advantage is considerable. With the aid of a small tactic, he can obtain an overwhelming position: **24.♗xd5! ♗xd5 25.♕f5! ♗e6 26.♖xe6! fxe6 27.♕xe6+ ♔h7 28.d5! ♕e7** (28...♘e7 29.♘b5) **29.♕f5+ g6 30.♕f4**.
In the game S.Guliev-Graf (Agios Nikolaos 1995), his love of the two bishops prevented White from playing the un-stereotyped exchange 24.♗xd5.
After the moves
24.♘xc4 ♘db4! 25.♗xb4 ♘xb4 26.cxb4 ♕xc4 27.♕xc4 ♗xc4 28.d5 ♔f8 29.♖c1 ♗b3 30.♖c7 a5 31.bxa5 bxa5 32.♖c5 ♖a8
(32...♗xa4!? 33.♖xa5 ♗b3+=)
33.d6 ♖d8 34.♖xa5 ♖xd6 35.♗f3 ♖d2 36.♖a7
(36.h4!?)
36...g5 37.a5 ♖a2 38.♔g2 ♗e6 39.h3 ♔g7 40.a6 ♗c4 41.♗b7 h5 42.♔f3 h4 43.♖a8 ♗e6 44.♔g2
a position was reached where White has an extra pawn, but it is not clear how he can exploit it.

One should respect the two bishops, but not worship them. – David Bronstein

Botvinnik considered that one of the reasons for the superiority of two bishops was the fact that, at the necessary moment, one of them can be exchanged.

Conclusion: During a game, do not be afraid to change the character of the position, replacing one type of advantage with another.

Solution 56

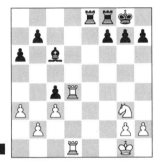

It is not hard to see that Black has a large advantage. More than that: he has a winning position! He can organise harmonious cooperation between his rooks and bishop. In the game Vorobiov-L.Guliev (Moscow 1995), correctly assessing the position and choosing the correct plan, Black quickly decided the outcome of the game in his favour.

1...f5! 2.♖xc4?! f4 3.♘f1 f3 4.gxf3 ♗xf3 5.♖d7 ♗e2 6.♖cc7 ♖xf1+ 7.♔g2 ♔h8! 8.♖d2 ♖ff8

And White resigned.

It can happen that a pawn, supported by a colleague, can develop a strength greater than that of a piece!

If you rub shoulders with a good man, then, like a copper coin rubbing against a silver one, you will come out of it in a much enhanced state. – Maxim Gorky

Solution 57

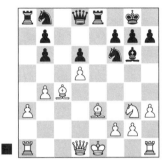

If the game proceeds normally and White succeeds in castling, then his position will be clearly better, as he has the two bishops and a lead in development.

Understanding this, Black in the game S.Guliev-Papaioannou (Agios Nikolaos 1995) decided to complicate play by means of

16...♘h5?

but after

17.♘xh5 ♖xe3+

(17...♕h4!?)

18.fxe3 ♕h4+ 19.g3! ♕xh5

(19...♕xc4 20.♖c1)

20.♕xh5 ♗xh5 21.♗b5

White obtained a winning position. Thus, we can conclude that White is better in the starting position. Black should have chosen one of the following continuations:

16...♘bd7 or **16...♘e4 17.♘xe4 ♖xe4 18.♗e2 ♘d7**, settling for the fact that his position is worse and that he needs to go over to defence. It should be noted that Black has fully realistic chances of organising a satisfactory defence.

101

Conclusion: Attacks with sacrifices are always tempting, but at the same time require accurate calculation of variations and objective assessment.

There is nothing more exhilarating than to be shot at with no result. – Winston Churchill

Conclusion: In chess, the centre is the most important thing, but never forget about the flanks!

Look at the flanks whilst thinking of the centre – that is the highest form of positional play. – Aron Nimzowitsch

Solution 59

Solution 58

White's central set-up looks very good. But his king position creates serious worry, because the a2-square is weak. Close examination of the position teaches us that the ♖a6, the queen and the knight can all attack this weak spot. A player with sharp tactical vision will already be able to see it all and will not be deceived: Black is winning!
In the game Galkin-S.Guliev (Azov 1995) there followed:
29...♗xe5! 30.♕d3
He cannot save himself with either 30.♘xe5 ♖xa2+! 31.♔b1 ♘c3+ 32.♔c2 ♖xb2+! 33.♔xb2 ♕a2+ or 30.♖xe5 ♘c3.
30...b5! 31.♘xe5 ♖xa2+!?
Even stronger was 31...♘c3! 32.♘xc6+ ♔a8.
32.♔b1 ♘c3+ 33.♔c1 ♖a1+
White resigned.

On the queenside, White is ready to carry out the typical Carlsbad structure plan of a 'minority attack'. In response, Black has organised a pawn attack on the kingside and will seize every possibility to hinder White's play on the other wing. Here in the game Mikhailov-S.Guliev (Kazan 1995) Black strengthened his position with an unusual manoeuvre and at the same time stopped his opponent's queenside offensive:
21...♖c8! 22.♗f1 ♖c7! 23.♘c5 ♗c8 24.♗d3 ♘e4 25.♘xe4? fxe4 26.♗e2 h4 27.♔g2 ♕h5!
And Black obtained a very strong attack. It is said that for a great performer to show what he is capable of, he needs a big arena. In chess, rooks need open lines!

Where there is no space to show one's capabilities, there are no capabilities. – Ludwig Feuerbach

Solution 60

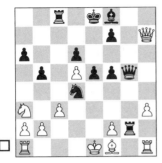

The position is characteristic of the Chelyabinsk/Sveshnikov Variation of the Sicilian. Black's position is winning.

The reader should especially study the position arising after:

19.♗xg2 ♕xg2 20.0-0-0

Now in L.Guliev-Rogozenco (Nikolaev 1995) Black decided on

20...b4!

To tell the truth, there was nothing stronger, e.g.

   A) 20...♕xf2 21.♖hf1 ♕e3+ 22.♔b1;

   B) 20...♕e4 21.♖he1; or

   C) 20...♕g5+ 21.♔b1 ♘f3 22.♘c2 etc.

These continuations promise Black nothing.

21.♘c2 bxc3

21...♘xc2 22.♕xf5!.

22.♘xd4 ♕xf2

22...♕g5+ 23.♔c2.

23.bxc3 ♖xc3+

23...exd4! decides the game.

24.♔b1 exd4?

Correct was 24...♖a3 25.♘c2 ♖xa2! 26.♔xa2 ♕xc2+ with perpetual check. 26.♖c1? looks dangerous because of 26...♖a4! and the white king cannot defend against the numerous threats.

It was this exact variation that should have led the game to a draw, but Black played differently!

25.♖he1+! ♖e3 26.♖f1 ♕g2 27.♕xf5 ♕e4+ 28.♕xe4+ ♖xe4 29.♖de1 ♖e5 30.♔c2 ♔e7 31.♔d3 ♗g7 32.♖xe5+ dxe5 33.d6+ ♔xd6 34.♖xf7 ♗h8 35.♔e4 ♔c5 36.h4

And White won.

In this game, White showed excellent defensive quality. He evidently remembered the words of a wise expert on the subject:

Defence requires manliness and great tenacity. – Emanuel Lasker

But to Black, who started by attacking cleverly and then hesitated halfway, one can address the words of another chess genius:

A direct and energetic attack on the king is successful when all of the pieces take part, all available forces. Resistance must be overcome at all costs. The attack cannot be halted halfway, since this usually leads to defeat. – José Raul Capablanca

Conclusion: Don't be afraid to throw wood onto the fire!

Solution 61

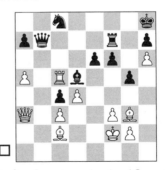

White's advantage is significant. He has two bishops, he controls greater space, and the h6-pawn restricts the enemy king's mobility.

Together these factors allow White to land a decisive tactical blow.
42.♖c7!
After this simple deflection move, in the game S.Guliev-Grechikin (Moscow 1995), Black had nothing left other than to stop the clocks.

Conclusion: One must not allow the opponent to obtain superiority on all lines of the front.

There can be no combination without a significant superiority and no significant superiority without a combination. – Emanuel Lasker

Solution 62

In the game L.Guliev-Lundin (Moscow 1995), White's last move 1.♘c3-e4 deliberately provoked Black into an active jump, setting a trap. And it worked! Black did not believe his opponent. There followed:
1...♘cb4? 2.axb4 ♘xb4 3.♕b5! ♘xc2 4.♕e5 f6 5.♕xe6+ ♔h8 6.♕f7
The white queen fearlessly occupies all the squares formerly patrolled by the black pieces and decides the outcome of the game.
Be wary of letting the enemy's strongest piece develop such great activity!

6...♖g8 7.♖xa7 ♖c7 8.♖xb7
Even stronger was 8.♗f4! with the idea of 8...♖d7 9.♘eg5!.
8...♖xb7 9.♘xf6 ♗xf6 10.♕xb7 ♘xd4 11.♖a1 ♘xf3+ 12.gxf3 ♗g7 13.♖a7 ♕f6 14.b3 g5 15.♗xg7+ ♖xg7 16.♕xg7+ ♕xg7 17.♖a8+ ♕g8 18.♖xg8+ ♔xg8 19.♔g2 ♔f7 20.♔g3 ♔g6 21.f4
And White soon won.

Conclusion: It is extremely important to be precise!

Do not be fooled if your opponent suddenly leaves a pawn undefended or otherwise offers you some obvious advantage. More often than not it will be a trap, which in the heat of battle can be easy to fall into. – Viacheslav Dydyshko

Solution 63

At first glance, White has the advantage. It seems that Black must play 25...♘d5 26.♘xc4 with an obvious superiority. But tactics come to Black's aid! The position is roughly equal.
In the game S.Guliev-Shabanov (Moscow 1995) Black managed to change the course of the game with an exchange sacrifice, obtaining sufficient compensation and then

even the advantage, after a mistake by White:

25...♖xe4! 26.♘xe4 ♘xf5 27.♘d6 ♘xd6 28.♗xd6 ♕d5 29.♗c5?
Correct was 29.♗xf8! with roughly equal chances.
29...♘e6 30.♕b7 ♖d8 31.♕xa7 ♘f4!
Black's superiority is already indisputable.

Conclusion: Abruptness can also be an advantage.

It is well-known that the real difficulty lies not in calculation, but in assessing the position after an exchange sacrifice. – Efim Geller

Solution 64

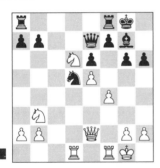

Euwe, in his book *The Middle Game*, pointed out that a knight on the third rank is good for defence, especially blockade; a knight on the fourth rank can be good for both defence and attack; a knight on the fifth rank generally has good potential for attack, and a knight on the sixth rank will usually guarantee its side an advantage sufficient to win.
In the diagram, White's knight is already on the sixth, and he needs only to strengthen this outpost. As soon as his other pieces can support

this knight, White's pressure will become irresistible. In the game Zakharevich-S.Guliev (Moscow 1995), in order to prevent such a turn of events, Black turned to the universal medicine – tactics! Thanks precisely to this possibility, the position is roughly equal:
21...♖ad8 22.g3 ♖xd6! 23.exd6 ♕xd6 24.♖d2 ♖c8 25.♕b5 b6 26.♖c1 ♖d8 27.♕a4 a5
And here the strong knight on d5, the extra pawn and the weakened white king mean that Black has full compensation for the exchange. He even has some initiative, because it is not so easy to bring the ♘b3 into play.

Conclusion: First envy, then improvise!

Pay attention to your thoughts, they are the beginning of actions. – Lao Tzu

Solution 65

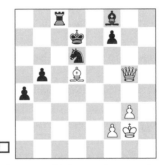

This is one of the easier tactical puzzles for the amateur to solve. Black has a small material deficit. If his pieces could achieve harmony, it would not be easy for White to realise his advantage.
In the game L.Guliev-Milov (Nikolaev 1995) White found the

quickest way to end his opponent's resistance:

57.♗xf7! ♘xf7 58.♕f5+ ♔d8

Possibly more tenacious was 58...♔c7 59.♕xf7+ ♔b6.

59.♕xf7 ♗c5 60.♕d5+ ♔e8 61.♕b7 ♔d8 62.♕xb5 a3 63.g4 ♖c7 64.♕a5 ♔d7 65.g5

And White's position is easily winning.

Conclusion: Solve plenty of combinations, both simple and difficult.

Like muscles, every skill needs training. – A.V.Obruchev

Solution 66

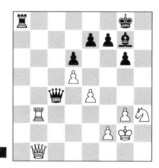

Black's position is clearly better. The more active queen, compact pawn structure and the poor position of the ♘h3 underline this assessment. Maybe Black should have chosen the unhurried 33...♗f6!?, retaining all the advantages of his position. However, in the game S.Guliev-Ivanov (Moscow 1995) Black decided the time had come to go over to active operations and he played:

33...♖a1?

After this the game should end in a draw. White has a tactical possibility:

34.♖b8+ ♔h7 35.♘g5+ ♔h6 36.♘xf7+ ♔h5?

He should have repeated with 36...♔h7, and White has nothing but perpetual check. Black evidently overlooked his opponent's next two moves.

37.♖b4! ♕a6?

Black still doesn't understand what is happening. He should have settled for 37...♖xb1 38.♖xc4 g5.

38.e5!

And in view of the threat of mate by 39.♖h4, Black resigned.

Conclusion: Better a bird in the hand than two in the bush.

It is necessary to calculate the end of all things and how everything turns out; God gives many people a glimpse of prosperity, only to tear up their lives by the roots. – Herodotus

Solution 67

This position requires a dynamic approach. So as to assess such a situation correctly, one needs to be able to calculate variations with great accuracy. This allows us to draw the conclusion: the game is equal.

In the game L.Guliev-Vaulin (Moscow 1995) there followed:

41...罩d8!
and the players agreed a draw because of the variations 42.營xd8 罩a4+ 43.含b3 罩b4+ 44.含c3 (44.含a2 罩a4+=) 44...營e3+ 45.罩d3 (45.營d3?? 營c5+) 45...營e1+ 罩cd2 營c1+. As we see, White cannot avoid perpetual check.

Conclusion: Believe in defensive resources!

When the strategic battle is lost, one must rely on tactical traps. –Eduard Gufeld

Solution 68

White controls the centre and he also has a territorial advantage on the queenside. On the other hand, Black has no weaknesses. His main problem is his lack of space. In such a situation, the attacking side tries to suffocate his opponent, whilst the defender must patiently await his moment, trying not to allow himself to be completely suffocated, and at the first opportunity go over to a counterattack.
By means of **15...a5! 16.bxa5** (16. b5? cxb5 17.axb5 罩fc8) **16...②c8! 17.②c4 ②d6** (and on 18.營f4?? there is 18...g5!) Black could free his position and equalise. If you found this manoeuvre, you have a good feeling for the turning points in the game and understand when it is necessary to wait and when to act. But if you missed this and instead preferred
15...罩ad8
as in the game Kiselev-S.Guliev (Moscow 1995), then after
16.營c2 e5?! 17.dxe5 營xe5 18.a5 ②c8 19.②e3 ②f6? 20.罩ab1 營b5 21.f4
you could find yourself in a difficult position.
Specialists believe that if a temperamental player is offered 100 dubious positions that require active play, he will score more points than from 100 sound positions requiring passive, waiting tactics. And the opposite is the case for a less temperamental player. So, the player's character has a serious, if not decisive effect when playing non-standard positions.

Conclusion: The character of a person is manifested in his actions.

Patience is a good quality, but life is too short to exercise much patience. – Abdul Faraj

Solution 69

Probably many of you could hardly believe your eyes, as this test seems so easy. What can one do? Dear reader, real strength lies in simplicity.

35...♘g3! 36.♖e1

After 36.hxg3 hxg3 there is no normal means to stop the mate threat.

36...♘e4 37.♕d3 ♘xd2

And in the game Bezman-S.Guliev (Moscow 1995) White resigned.

Conclusion: Simplicity never deceives one!

The hardest questions to answer are the obvious ones. – George Bernard Shaw

Solution 70

Another easy example to test your combinative vision. All White's pieces are taking part in the assault. In such positions, it is very important not to allow the pace of the attack to slacken, and not to miss the key moments which require decisive action.

In the game L.Guliev-Smugalev (Moscow 1995) White achieved success by means of:

26.♗h6!

After

26...gxh6

(26...♘e6 27.♖xe6)

27.♘f6+ ♔f8 28.♘xh7+ ♔g8
29.♘f6+ ♔f8 30.♘xe8 ♘xd7
31.♖xd7 ♔xe8 32.♖c7

Black resigned, since there is no defence against mate.

Conclusion: Superiority in the centre and on the seventh rank often has decisive significance.

When all the pieces are working, there definitely should be a solution to the position. – Gennady Nesis, Leonid Shulman

Solution 71

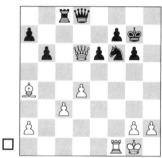

The position is very complicated. However, White has the tempting possibility of pinning the ♘f6. The assessment of the position depends to a large degree on the effectiveness of this pin. How dangerous is it for Black? Strong tacticians and players familiar with combinational motifs will be in no doubt: White is better! The game S.Guliev-Baikov (Moscow 1995) continued

31.♕e5! ♖xc3

and now 32.♗b3! is a very important nuance (the immediate 32.g4? ♖c4 favours Black). After 32...a5 33.g4 a4 34.♗d1 ♖c4 35.g5 White is better.

Play continued with

32.♗b5

but after

32...♖a3 33.g4

Black has 33...♖a5!∓ and ...a7-a6
next. Therefore, 33.h4 would have
been better. The idea is to make a
draw after 33...♖a5 34.a4 a6 35.h5!
gxh5 36.♕g5+ ♔f8 37.♕h6+ ♔g8
38.♕g5+.

However, after

33...a6 34.♗c6 ♖xa2 35.g5 ♖d2 36.d5!
(aiming to break through to the
f7-square; in the event of 36.♕xf6+
♕xf6 37.gxf6+ ♔h6 or 36.♖xf6
♕xd4+ 37.♕xd4 ♖xd4, Black retains
some chances, despite his piece
deficit)

36...exd5 37.♖xf6 ♔g8 38.♗e8

Black soon resigned.

Conclusion: Which forms of pin do
you know?

*Sporadic cases of pinning (or even the
threat thereof) can force the opponent to
make moves which weaken the position,
and thereby have an effect on the whole
game, right down to its final stages! –*
Aron Nimzowitsch

Solution 72

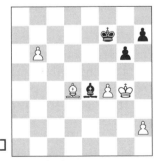

We have an endgame with opposite-
coloured bishops. This always

promises the weaker side additional
drawing chances. In such positions,
even several extra pawns often fail
to suffice for a win.

For a long time, White could not
find the winning method in the
game S.Guliev-Frog (Moscow 1995).
Then he found the following plan:
transfer the king to g5 and the
bishop to the diagonal d8-h4, after
which there follows the exchange
of the f- and g-pawns (by means
of f4-f5), and the king can advance
by force to c7, winning the bishop.
Carrying out this plan, White wins.

48.♔g5 ♗b7 49.♗f2!

49.f5? gxf5 50.♔xf5 ♔e7 51.♔g5 ♔d7
52.♔h6 ♗e4 and then the king goes
via c8 to b7, securing a draw.

49...♔g7

Standing on the spot gives Black
good drawing chances: 49...♗c6
50.♔h6!? ♔g8.

50.f5! ♔f7

50...gxf5 51.♔xf5 ♔f7 52.♗h4! ♔e8
53.♔e6 and then ♔e6-d6-c7.

51.♗h4! ♗c8

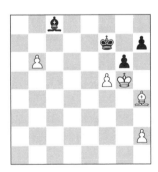

52.f6

52.fxg6+? hxg6 53.♔f4 ♔e6, and
the black king goes to b7, achieving
a draw. However, 52.♔h6 wins
immediately!

52...♗b7 53.♔h6

53.♗f4 ♔e6 54.♗g5 h6! 55.♗h4
♗a8! (55...g5+? 56.♗xg5 hxg5+
57.♔xg5 ♔f7 58.h4 ♗c6 59.h5 ♗b7
60.h6 ♔g8 61.♔f5! followed by
♔f5-e6-e7 and wins) 56.♔e3 g5=.
**53...♔g8 54.♗g5 ♗a8 55.h4 ♗b7
56.h5! gxh5??**

56...♗e4 seems to make a draw.

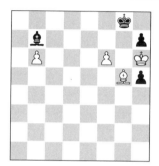

57.♗h4

The aim of the last few moves was
to free the g5-square, so the king
can reach c7.

57...♗c8 58.♔xh5 ♔f7 59.♔g5 ♔e6

Black is in zugzwang: 59...♗b7
60.♔f5!; 59...♗d7 60.b7; 59...♔f8
60.♔f4 and ♔e5.

60.♔h6!!

After 60.♔f4 ♗b7 61.♔e3 ♗a8
62.♔d4 ♗h1 63.♔c5 ♗b7! 64.♔b5
♔f7! 65.♔c5 ♔e6 White would have
to return the king to h6 and carry
out the necessary triangulation,
to win a tempo and thus seize the
key square f5. Now, however, this
technical device is effected at once.

60...♔f7

60...♗b7 61.♔g7.

61.♔xh7 ♗b7

Freeing the g6-square; this is of
decisive significance, since with the
king on g5, Black does not have the
move ...♔e6.

**62.♔h6 ♗e4 63.♔h5 ♔e6 64.♔g5
♔d7**

And now, without waiting for
65.♔h6 and then 66.♔g7 or 65.f7
♔e7 66.♔f4+, Black resigned.

Conclusion: With only a few pieces
on the board, creative play requires
great artistry, which is why it is
so difficult to play such 'simple'
positions.

*Without a deep knowledge of the
endgame, one cannot hope to play
successfully in strong tournaments. –
Georgy Lisitsin*

Solution 73

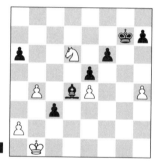

Black has the clear intention to
penetrate on the kingside with
...♔g7-g6-h5. In the game Bologan–
L.Guliev (Moscow 1995) White's
last two moves were 1.c2-c4 bxc3
2.b3-b4. With the pawn sacrifice,
he established good chances of
organising a passed pawn on the
queenside. In this way, White has
seriously enlivened the game.
There is play on both flanks. In
such situations, the bishop is
usually stronger than the knight.
This position is no exception. Black
has the advantage. Thanks to the
activity of the black king and the
weakness of the h4-pawn, this
advantage will soon become clear.

2...♔g6 3.a4 ♔h5 4.♘f5 ♔g4
5.♘xd4?!
More tenacious was 5.♔c2 ♔f4
6.♘d6! (6.b5 axb5 7.axb5 ♗c5 8.♔d3
c2 9.♔xc2 ♔xe4) 6...h5! 7.b5 axb5
8.axb5 ♗f2, although here too,
Black has a clear advantage.
5...exd4 6.b5
6.♔c2 ♔f3 7.♔d3 c2! 8.♔d2 d3 9.b5
c1♕+ 10.♔xc1 ♔e2+−.
6...axb5 7.axb5 d3 8.b6 ♔f3 9.b7
d2 10.♔c2 ♔e2 11.b8♕ d1♕+
12.♔xc3 ♕d3+ 13.♔b2 ♕xe4
14.♕b5+ ♔e1 15.♕a5+ ♔f1
And Black soon won.

Conclusion: In the endgame, the
king is an important piece!

*... a pawn sacrifice can often be deeper
than a piece sacrifice. – Siegbert
Tarrasch*

Solution 74

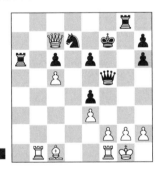

Black appears to have a very
difficult position. In the game
S.Guliev-Kholmov (Moscow 1995)
White, in playing ♕f4-c7, was
convinced that he had a large
advantage.
As he sat there dreaming happily
about how to convert his advantage,
Black played:
24...♖a7!!

This move came like lightning out
of a clear sky for White! He thought
for a long time, but could find
nothing better than
25.♕xa7
(very dangerous is 25.♕d6 ♘e5),
settling for a draw after
**25...♖xg2+ 26.♔xg2 ♕g4+ 27.♔h1
♕f3+**
In the 1960s, Ratmir Kholmov
was one of the top GMs. He was
especially noted for his defensive
skill in difficult positions, which
earned him the nickname 'the
Central Defender'. This example
shows that his reputation was fully
deserved.

Conclusion: When it seems to
you that the opponent is in an
inescapable position, be extra
careful!

*... you need to have a special defensive
plan. – Alexander Kotov*

Solution 75

The position is drawn! To show
that this is the case, Black must
organise contact between his queen
on a2 and his rook and bishop at
the rear of his position. The role of
communicator goes to the bishop.
1...♗f4+! 2.♔d1

2.gxf4? ♖g1+, or 2.♗e3 ♗xe3+
3.♕xe3 ♕xd5 with advantage to
Black.
2...♕b1+ 3.♔e2 ♕b5+ 4.♔e1 ♕b1+
With perpetual check. After a few
more moves in the game Ivanov-L.
Guliev (Moscow 1995) the players
agreed a draw.

Conclusion: Harmonious
cooperation between the pieces is
essential.

Solution 76

Here the question posed seems a
simple one. Which are stronger,
White's knights or Black's bishops?
In reality, this question often
seems simple but can be quite
complicated. For readers familiar
with the famous games Paulsen-
Tarrasch (Nuremberg 1888) and
Spassky-Pomar (Leiden 1970),
and who remember the subtle
manoeuvres ♕d3-a3 (...♕a7-a6)
which occurred in those games, our
question here should not prove too
difficult. Black has the advantage.
In the game Zakharov-S.Guliev
(Moscow 1995) Black played:
15...♕a6!
Widening the front. With this
move, he shifts the weight of the
battle to the queenside. Now the

powerful position of the knight on
d4 is already not so significant in
the further play. There followed
**16.♕xa6 bxa6 17.♖bd1 ♖ab8 18.♖d2
a5 19.♖e1 a4 20.a3 ♖b6 21.♖ee2
♖cb8 22.♘e1?! ♗g5 23.♖c2 ♗c8!**
with the threat of 24...♗a6!, and
Black obtained a winning position.

Conclusion: Again, the eternal
question: which is stronger, bishop
or knight?

*Eternal questions have temporary
answers. – Robert Greene*

Solution 77

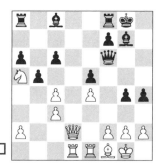

In the centre, White enjoys a
superiority. Black has replied with
a pawn storm on the kingside. In
the game S.Guliev-Cherniaev (St
Petersburg 1995) White faced a
dilemma: should he continue active
play in the centre with 22.♕d6 or
go for prophylaxis with 22.g3!?, first
strengthening his position on the
kingside and only then returning to
play in the centre? At the board, he
was too hasty!
22.♕d6? g3! 23.hxg3 hxg3 24.fxg3?
Better was 24.♕xf6 ♗xf6 25.♘xc6!
(25.fxg3 ♗e7!) 25...gxf2+ 26.♔xf2
♗e6, which leads to a double-edged
position.

24...♕g5! 25.♘xc6 ♕xg3 26.c5
More tenacious was 26.♘e7+ ♔h8
27.♕d3, settling for slightly better
play for Black.
26...♗e6! 27.♕d3?
Here too 27.♘e7+ ♔h8 28.♕d3 looks
stronger.
27...♕g5!
White now has a difficult position.
28.♖e3 ♖fc8! 29.♖g3 ♕h4 30.♘xe5?

30...♖d8 0-1
Over the course of several moves,
White spoiled a superior position
and then, upset by this, lost in a
few moves. In reality, he was better
at the start. With the prophylactic
move 22.g3! White should first
have prevented Black's kingside
counterplay, and then Black would
have faced serious problems.
King's Indian players consider that in
positions of this type, White should
slow up the enemy attack with g2-g3.
If this is played at the right moment,
White usually obtains the advantage.
This example shows that white
players should not try to mess with
the natural order of things!

Conclusion: Prophylaxis is the ability
to nip possible danger in the bud.

*Develop your ability to notice the smallest
of your problems and solve them before*

*they grow and get out of control. Learn
to distinguish between problems that can
lead to disaster, and simply annoying
troubles that can eventually be resolved
by themselves.* – Robert Greene, from
the book *The 48 Laws of Power*

Solution 78

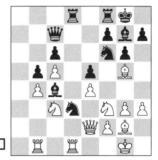

At a superficial glance, the ♘d3
is dangerous to White. However,
the attentive reader will already
have noticed that this knight has
no retreat squares and it is also
difficult to bring it any assistance!
White is winning.
In order to reveal the defects of
the black position, in the game
S.Guliev-Iskusnyh (Vladivostok
1995) it was enough to regroup the
white forces, which White managed
to do within four moves:
22.♕e3! ♖d7
There is no other defence against
23.♗f1.
23.♗f1 ♖fd8 24.♘h2!+−
The threat is 25.♕f3!.
24...♖d4
There is no obvious defence, but
maybe 24...h6!?.
25.♕f3! ♘e8 26.♗xd8 ♕xd8 27.♘e2
And White soon won.

Conclusion: Sometimes knights
can stray too far!

Insolence should be met with dignity. – Alexey Suetin

Solution 79

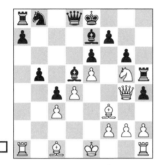

White is winning. In the game S.Guliev-Markov (Vladivostok 1995), after the move

1.♘xe6!

Black decided to surrender at once. Indeed, he has nothing to hope for, as is shown by the variations 1...fxe6 2.♕xg6+, 1...♗xe6 2.♕e4 or 1...♗xf3 2.gxf3 (or 2.♕xf3).

Conclusion: One must keep an eye on the enemy's active pieces.

If you do not manage to castle and your king gets trapped in the centre, the opponent will usually have very good chances of success. – Alexander Kotov

Solution 80

In the game Godzhaev-S.Guliev (Baku 1996) Black had just played 20...♖d8-d2 and was very satisfied with his position. However, the game is equal.
The calm white reply

21.♗b1!

came as a cold shower to Black. He thought for about an hour, but did not find anything. Admittedly, his thoughts were occupied not so much with the calculation of variations, as with attempts to calm himself down and come to terms with the fact that the advantage was gone and it was necessary to find a path to retain equality. In the end, he could find nothing better than the line below, which leads to a slightly better endgame for White.

21...♗b4?! 22.♗xb4 ♘xb4 23.a3 ♘d3

24.♘e4! ♘xc1 25.♘xd2 g6 26.b4 ♚g7 27.♘e4

And the game soon ended in a draw. In fact, securing equality requires precision from Black. It was worth considering 21...♘b4 22.♘e4 ♖e2! 23.♘c3 ♖d2 24.♘e4 and it is unfavourable for either side to avoid the repetition.

Conclusion: Surprises can be met anywhere!

Life always gives a man less than he demands from it. – Jack London

Solution 81

Black has two bishops and a promising position in the centre. But at the same time, the position of the black king and especially the queenside pawn structure are seriously weakened, and the latter factor is especially important. White has a winning position. He needs to shift the weight of the struggle to the queenside and attack the black weaknesses there.
In the game S.Guliev-Maharramzade (Baku 1996), with this in mind, White played
27.a4!
and after the moves
27...b4
(27...bxa4 28.♖c3+ ♔b8 29.♗xa6!)
28.c3! b3 29.♗d3!
Black fell into a very difficult position. There followed
29...♔b8 30.♗xa6! ♗f4 31.♖f3 ♖dg8 32.♕xf4 ♕xf4 33.♖xf4 ♗xa6 34.♖xf7 ♖xg2 35.♘xb3
and White achieved a technically winning position.

Conclusion: Do not forget that a rook works not only on files, but

also on ranks. Those familiar with the classic game Karpov-Hort (Moscow 1971) will recall this.

If a weakness cannot be attacked, then it does not matter. – Aron Nimzowitsch

Solution 82

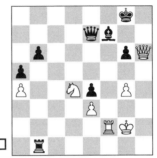

Yes, he was right. White's attack is very strong. It not only compensates for the pawn but even gives an advantage sufficient for victory, as Black did not respond adequately in the game S.Guliev-Shur (Baku 1996):
51.♘f5 ♕e5?
  A) No better was 51...gxf5 52.♖xf5 ♖b2+ 53.♔h3;
  B) A more tenacious defence was 51...♕f6 52.♖d2 ♗e8! (52...♖b2 53.♘e7+ ♕xe7 54.♖xb2; 52...♗d5 53.♖xd5 ♕b2+ 54.♔g3 ♖g1+ 55.♔f4 ♕f2+ 56.♔e5) 53.♖d8 ♕b2+ 54.♔g3 ♕e5+ and Black holds.
52.♕g5!
And in view of the variations
52...♔h7 53.♕h4+ ♔g8 54.♘h6+
or 52...♔f8 53.♕d8+ ♕e8 54.♕d6+ ♔g8 55.♘h6+ Black resigned.

Conclusion: Not only snakes are poisonous – pawns can be as well!

Solution 83

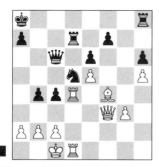

Thanks to the strong knight on d5, Black has managed to advance his queenside pawns and is now already threatening to attack the white king's residence. However, for this he has been forced to weaken his own monarch's position, and the h6-pawn is also weak. But since he is aiming at the white king, Black's position is better.

With the move **31...Rc8!**, creating the threat of 3...c3, Black could cement his superiority. The immediate 31...c3? fails to 32.Rxb4! Nxb4 33.Qxc6 Nxc6 34.Rxd7.

In the game Zulfugarli-S.Guliev (Baku 1996) Black momentarily lost his concentration and played

31...Rb7?

and White was practically forced (Black threatens 32...b3!) to sacrifice the exchange, but this gives him a serious initiative.

32.Rxd5! exd5 33.Qxd5 Qa6

33...Qc8!?.

34.e6 Qxe6 35.Qd8+ Qc8

36.Qxc8+ Rxc8 37.Bxh6 b3 38.axb3 cxb3 39.c3 Rb5 40.g4 Ra5 41.Bg7! Ra1+?!

After 41...Rg5! 42.h6 Rxg4 43.Rh1 Rg2 Black retains enough counterplay to hold the balance.

42.Kd2 Rd8+ 43.Bd4 Ra2??

The decisive mistake. He could still hold a draw with 43...Rxd1+ 44.Kxd1 f6!. But now White should win.

44.Rb1 f6 45.Ke3 Re8+ 46.Kf3 Rf8 47.h6

And soon Black resigned.

Conclusion: Important squares should be over-protected.

Prophylaxis is what we mean by preventive measures against moves which are positionally undesirable. – Aron Nimzowitsch

Solution 84

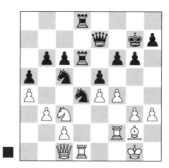

The black knights' hegemony in the centre and thereabouts ensures his superiority. But it is not easy to find a plan to increase the pressure on White. In the game Yuferov-L. Guliev (Moscow 1996) Black solved this problem tactically. He played a combination, in which he gives up the two knights for rook and pawn. Nominally, in the material sense he is even slightly worse off, but thanks to the weak position of the white king, his control of the d-file and the passive enemy minor pieces, Black gets the advantage. The game continued:

29...Ndxb3! 30.cxb3 Nd3 31.Rxd3

Or 31.♕e3!? ♘xf2 32.♖xd6 ♕xd6 (32...♘xh3+ 33.♗xh3 ♕xd6 34.♕xb6 ♕d2) 33.♕xf2 (33.♔xf2 ♕d2+ 34.♘e2 ♕xe3+ 35.♔xe3 ♖d1) 33...♕b4 34.♕c2 ♕d4+ 35.♔h2 ♕d2 with advantage to Black.

31...♖xd3 32.♔h2

32...♕d6!

A) Weaker was 32...♕c5?! 33.♖c2! ♕e3 34.♕xe3 ♖xe3 35.♗f1; or

B) 32...♕b4? 33.♘d5! ♕c5 (33...♕d6 34.♕c2) 34.♖c2.

33.fxe5 fxe5

33...♕xe5 34.♘e2 and then ♘f4.

34.♗f1 ♕d4 35.♖c2 ♖d2+! 36.♖xd2 ♕xd2+ 37.♕xd2 ♖xd2+ 38.♔g1 ♖c2 39.♘d1 ♖c1 40.♘e3 ♖c3 41.♘c4 ♖xg3+ 42.♔f2 ♖xb3 43.♘xe5 b5

43...♖b4 44.♘xc6 ♖xa4.

44.♘xc6 bxa4 45.♘xa5 ♖b2+

And White resigned.

It is generally accepted that, in the middlegame, two minor pieces are stronger than rook and pawn. But in the endgame, in many cases, especially when the player with the rook also has a passed pawn, then the rook and pawn can prove stronger. One should note in particular that everything depends on the specifics of each position. For players who understand these subtleties, the last exercise should have been a walk in the park.

One of the characteristics of modern chess is the analysis of positions with unbalanced material. For example, in the games of Mikhail Tal, one often comes across positions where a rook and a pawn battle against two minor pieces. In the games of Kasparov (and also Anand and Topalov), one often sees instances where a queen and pawns fight three minor pieces (or two minor pieces and rook). Here the position of the player without the queen is usually weakened. The queen is exchanged for two rooks most often in the games of Fischer.

This all leads one to the theory that various players study positions of this type, because to this day, there is no general theory of such material balances in the textbooks. Such issues as weak or strong squares, good or bad pieces, weak kings, etc. are no longer the leading matters in contemporary chess, although they remain fundamental to the game. Of course, they have to be studied, but you will not achieve any great successes only with a knowledge of these. Therefore, the top players of today in their researches into middlegame strategy tend to direct their energies more into non-standard positions.

Conclusion: How do you feel in positions with non-standard material balances?

Rook and two pawns are almost stronger than two minor pieces in the endgame... in the middlegame, the situation is somewhat different. Here one must reckon with the attacking possibilities of the opponent, and so there is usually not time to concern oneself with creating a passed pawn, for instance. – Alexander Panchenko

Solution 85

The position has a concrete character. Black is winning. After

17...exd5!

Black will at the very least emerge with an extra pawn.

18.♗xb6?! ♗d6!!

In the game Ivanov-L.Guliev (Moscow 1996) this move came as a bolt from the blue for White.

19.♗xa5 ♗xh2+ 20.♔h1 ♗f4+ 21.♔g1 ♗h2+ 22.♔h1 ♗f4+ 23.♔g1 d4!

A wonderful example of the strength of the two bishops.

24.♖fe1 ♕xa5 25.♖xd4 ♗xf3 26.gxf3 ♕g5+ 27.♔f1 ♕h5!

And Black's attack is unstoppable. Shamefully, we must admit that later, after a terrible blunder (helped by time-trouble), Black even lost! One cannot help remembering the words of the great ancient Greek philosopher:

Courage is the start of the action, but chance controls the outcome. – Democritus

Conclusion: You live and learn.

Solution 86

Black appears to have a clear advantage. He has an extra pawn and the white king position is seriously compromised – all these factors point to such an assessment. However, White has a fortunate fleeting chance! Exploiting it in the game L.Guliev-Zaitsev (Moscow 1996), White managed to equalise. The position is drawn.

30.dxc5! ♘xc5 31.♗xc5 ♗xc5 32.♗c4!

Probably Black had missed this nuance in his preliminary calculations.

32...♔h8 33.♗xd5 ♕b4 34.♕c4 ♕b6 35.♕c3 ♕a7 36.♖a1 ♕b6 37.♖a8 ♖xa8 38.♗xa8 ♕d6 39.♔g2 h5 40.♕f3 g6 ½-½

Conclusion: If you cannot eliminate your weaknesses, you need to try to make them such that the opponent cannot really exploit them.

Remember always that the regime of economy in art is always the most important rule of every production of aesthetic values. – Vladimir Mayakovsky

Solution 87

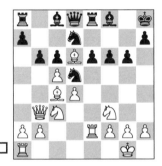

His large territorial superiority and piece activity ensures White's advantage. In the game L.Guliev-Genba (Moscow 1996) play continued

1.♗xd5!? exd5

More tenacious was 1...cxd5 2.♗xf8 ♘xf8 3.♘b5 with advantage.

2.♗c7! ♕xc7 3.♖xe8 bxc5 4.dxc5 ♔g7 5.♘a4 ♔f7 6.♖ae1 ♕a5 7.♕e3

And White soon won. Sometimes even the strongest pieces prove completely helpless, especially if time and conditions are against them.

Conclusion: Passive pieces present themselves as a chronic ailment whenever there is the slightest tension.

Any form of unprincipled behaviour eventually results in bankruptcy. – Johann Wolfgang von Goethe

Solution 88

The assessment of the position depends on the possibility of 18...♘d3+, since after 18...♘c6 19.0-0 ♗d7 20.♖e1 and then development along the lines of a2-a3, h2-h3, ♘g5, f2-f4, ♘e4 and ♘d6, White gets an obvious advantage.

18...♘d3+!

Yes, this move is possible, and it gives Black good chances to play for a win. The game Velicka-S.Guliev (Cappelle-la-Grande 1996) went as follows:

19.♔e2 b5!

One of the key moves.

20.♖xc8?!

Now Black's advantage becomes decisive. White faces a difficult life after:

A) 20.♖d4 ♘xb2 21.♗xd5 exd5 22.♖xd5 ♗e6!; or

B) 20.♖c2 ♘3f4+ 21.♔f1 ♗b7!; but

C) 20.♖g4 is slightly better for White: 20...h5 (20...♘xb2 21.♗h6!) 21.♖g3.

20...♘3f4+ 21.♗xf4 ♘xf4+ 22.♔e3 ♘xg2+ 23.♔e4 ♖axc8 24.♖g1 a5!

Also a key move.

25.♖xg2 a4 26.♗d1 ♖fd8!

119

Yet another important move in the variation.

27.♗e2

27.♖g1 ♖c1 28.♗e2 ♖c2!.

27...♖c2! 28.♗xb5 ♖xb2 29.♗d3 ♖xa2 30.♔e3 ♖a1 31.♖g4 ♖a8!

And Black soon won.

I can reveal that this was the longest variation the player of the black pieces had ever managed to calculate in a tournament game (from 18...♘d3+ to 29...♖xa2). Anyone who has played at Cappelle-la-Grande will know that after each round, the players are taken back to the hotel in buses. On the evening of this game, I happened to be sitting next to the highly respected GM, Vitaly Tseshkovsky. He asked me about the game and said that he had also calculated the whole of the key variation (we were playing on adjacent boards). He added that it was relatively easy to calculate because there were no side-variations. I must admit that I was very flattered that such a remarkable player should have taken such an interest in my game. That night, I had great trouble getting to sleep...

Conclusion: In the mouth of aces, the most ordinary words sound special!

Control all variations. Play the cards you are dealt. – Robert Greene

Solution 89

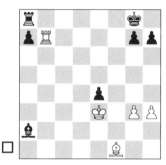

The position is drawn. In the game S.Guliev-Belikov (Moscow 1996) after the moves

31.♗a6! ♗e6 32.♖e7 ♗xh3 (32...♗d5 33.♖d7! ♗b3 34.♔xe4) **33.♗c4+ ♔h8 34.♗d5 ♖d8 35.♖xa7 ♗f5 36.♗xe4 ♖e8 37.♖a8**

a theoretically drawn position was reached. After the continuations 31.♗g2?! a5! 32.♗xe4 ♖e8! 33.♔d4 a4 34.♖a7 ♗b3 35.♗d5+ ♗xd5 36.♔xd5 ♖e3 or 31.♔xe4 a5 and then ...a5-a4 and ...♗b3, White would face serious problems.

Conclusion: Activity and again, activity!

The early bird catches the worm!

Solution 90

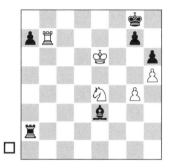

Yes, it compensates fully. In the game Samoliuk-S.Guliev (Moscow 1996) White ended the game nicely:
36.♘f6+! gxf6 37.♖b8+ ♔g7 38.♖b7+ ♔g8 39.♖b8+
With perpetual check.

Conclusion: How often have you regretted preferring material over activity?

Thus the eternal creative argument: material or the initiative? – Garry Kasparov

Solution 91

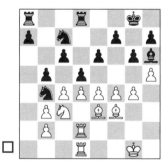

White, who has two bishops, has the advantage. In accordance with the classical canons of chess, he has advanced his pawns as far as possible to gain space (without putting the pawns themselves in danger), creating the conditions for the bishops to work more actively. Now he needs to open the game and use his pieces to support the advanced pawns.

In the game S.Guliev-Drozdov (Moscow 1996), by means of **23.hxg6 fxg6 24.cxd5 cxd5 25.♖h2! ♗f8 26.e5! a5 27.♘e2! a4 28.bxa4 bxa4 29.f5!**

White exploited the superiority of his position and went over to a strong attack. There followed: **29...a3 30.bxa3 ♖xa3 31.♗g5 ♖d7 32.♖f1 ♘c6 33.♗f6! exf5 34.gxf5 gxf5 35.♖g2+ ♗g7 36.♖c1! ♖a6 37.♘f4**

White's large advantage is obvious. **37...♔f8 38.♗xd5 ♘xd5 39.♗xg7+ ♔e7**

39...♖xg7 40.♘e6+.

40.♗f6+ ♘xf6 41.♖g7+ ♔e8 42.exf6 ♖xg7+ 43.fxg7 ♔f7 44.d5 ♘d8 45.♖c7+ ♔g8 46.♖c8 ♖d6 47.♘h5

And Black resigned.

The first to speak about the superiority of two bishops was the first World Champion, Wilhelm Steinitz. He worked out the method of play for the player with the bishops. The essence of this method is that, by advancing his pawns along the whole front, the stronger side takes away squares from the short-stepping knights of the opponent. – Alexander Panchenko

Conclusion: Do you have a special notebook of important practical positions and analyses, where we meet the advantage of the two bishops?

Solution 92

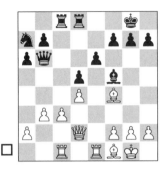

White has two bishops. How should he play, so they will be felt?
In the game S.Guliev-Iskusnyh (Moscow 1996) White played:
20.f3!
In this way, White attacks the enemy bishop, which is cut off from its other forces. He advances his pawns with tempo – at first on the kingside, and then on the other flank, seizing space for the successful use of his bishops.
20.♗e3 with the idea of ♗g3 is also decent for White.
There followed:
20...♗g6 21.g4 f6 22.♔h1 ♖e8 23.h4 ♘c6 24.♗e3
Also interesting was 24.h5 ♗f7 25.♗d3 and then ♖g1 and g4-g5.
24...♕c7 25.c4 ♖cd8 26.cxd5 exd5 27.h5 ♗f7 28.♔g2
White's space advantage is already obvious.
28...♖d7
Stronger was 28...♕b6.
29.♗f4 ♕b6 30.♖xe8+ ♗xe8 31.♖c5 ♗f7 32.♕c3 ♖e7 33.a3 ♖e8 34.b4 ♘d8 35.♗c7
35.♖c8!?.
35...♕e6 36.♗xd8 ♖xd8 37.♗d3 g6 38.h6!?
38.hxg6!?.

38...f5?! 39.gxf5 gxf5 40.♕c1! ♕d6 41.♗xf5 ♔h8 42.♕g5 ♗g6 43.♖xd5!
And Black resigned.

Conclusion: One must carefully study the different ways of exploiting the two bishops in positions with a space advantage.

If the front door to the hall is open, avoid the back door. – Henrik Ibsen

Solution 93

An extra pawn, well-placed and coordinated pieces, a strong passed c-pawn and the weakened position of the white king all allow us to conclude that Black has a winning position! Thanks to his two bishops, White has certain chances of attack, but at the moment, these have come to nothing. Now it is time for Black to begin his attack!
In the game Belikov-L.Guliev (Moscow 1996) Black quickly won, by combining the advance of the c-pawn with an attack on the white king.
32...c4 33.♗f4 ♖6d7 34.♗e8
White, in order somehow to sustain the flame of his attack, tries a regrouping of his forces, but it is too late.
34...♖g7+ 35.♔h3?! ♘f3! 36.♖f1 ♘g1+ 37.♖xg1 ♖xg1 38.♗g6 ♖d7

39.♖h6 c3! 40.♗e8 ♖d3+ 41.♔g3 ♖dxg3+! 42.hxg3 ♖h1+ 0-1

Conclusion: Chess has many positions in which one does not need to calculate long variations in order to find the correct plan or best move. But how can one identify these positions?

We think in generalities, but live in specifics. – Alfred North Whitehead

Solution 94

Black's position is better. The reason is the unfortunate white knight, trapped in the enemy position.
After
1...♖b6!
in the game Galdunts-L.Guliev (Moscow 1996) White could not cope with his emotions and blundered:
2.♖fd1?
Correct was 2.♘e4 ♘xe4 3.♖xe4 ♖d8 (or 3...♖c6), settling for the fact that Black has some advantage, thanks to his control of the d-file. Now, however, Black wins a pawn, thanks to the fork.
2...♖xd6! 3.♖xd6 ♘e4 4.♕d4
4.♕b6? ♕xb6 5.♖xb6 ♘f2+.
4...♘xd6 5.♕xd6 ♕xc2

And after a long battle, Black realised his extra pawn.

Conclusion: Look out carefully for any chance to land a fork, especially with a knight!

The ability to wait perhaps consists only in the ability to prevent small mistakes becoming bigger ones. – E.Bogat

Solution 95

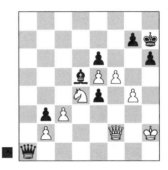

In positions where the players have castled on opposite sides, in the great majority of cases the outcome depends on which side first begins the attack. The attacking side dictates the conditions of the game.

It is obligatory to act more or less aggressively, as soon as given the chance. The initiative should be seized at the first opportunity. The initiative is an advantage. – José Raul Capablanca

The present position is just such an example. It occurred in the game Zaitsev-L.Guliev (Moscow 1996). If it were White's move, he would be able to turn the scales in his favour with 1.fxe6. But it is Black to move! This fact gives him a large advantage.
1...e3! 2.♕e2 ♕h1+ 3.♔g3

And now after 3... ♕g1+! 4.♔h3 (4.♔h4 ♕f2+) 4...♕f2! there is no defence against the threat of 5...♗g2+ and 6...♗f3+.

In the game, however, Black left the main path. Instead of 3...♕g1+ he played

3...♕e4?!

but in time-trouble, after mutual errors and adventures, he won all the same:

4.♘xe6 ♗c4 5.♕f3 ♕b1?! 6.g5?

6.♕xe3!.

6...♕g1+ 7.♔f4 ♕f2 8.g6+ ♔h8

etc.

There are heroes among the lower ranks, too. – Alexander Suvorov

The soldierly heroism of the e3-pawn in this example inevitably reminds one of the great commander's words.

The player with the initiative is obliged to develop it actively, otherwise it will pass to the opponent. – Wilhelm Steinitz

Conclusion: Bravery is a state of mind, not a matter of titles.

Solution 96

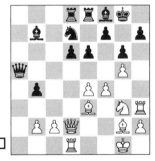

We have before us a typical Sicilian position, where White usually

attacks on the kingside and Black tries to organise counterplay in the centre and on the queenside. The white pieces are better mobilised (especially on the kingside), and so his position is preferable. In the game L.Guliev-Dragomaretsky (Moscow 1996) White chose an original path:

23.♘h1!!

Before the decisive battle, White regroups his forces. The knight transfers to g4 and the queen to f2.

23...♗g7

Possibly he should have tried to open play in the centre with 23...f5!?, exploiting the temporary absence of the knight from the game.

24.♘f2 ♗xb2

White has sacrificed a pawn, with the aim of improving the positions of his pieces. Perhaps Black should have declined and tried to prevent White from implementing his plan with 24...f5.

25.♘g4 ♗g7

Now 25...f5 is dangerous because of 26.exf5 ♗xg2 27.♘h6+.

26.♕f2

White's attack takes on a dangerous character. The threat is 27.♕h4, after which it is not obvious how Black can defend. Therefore he sacrifices the exchange, trying to transfer play to the centre and at the same time deflect White from the kingside.

26...f5 27.gxf6 ♘xf6 28.♘xf6+ ♗xf6 29.♗b6 ♕a8 30.♗xd8 ♖xd8

31.♕g3?

Although White has an extra exchange and the better game, the position remains very complicated since Black has a pawn and the two bishops. White needs to be accurate.

A) For example, the variation 31.e5? dxe5 32.♖xd8+ ♗xd8 33.♗xb7 (33.fxe5? ♕a1+! 34.♗f1 ♕a5!–+) 33...♕xb7 and ...♗b6 next favours Black;

B) White should have played 31.f5!, after which he is better.

31...♕c8

Black could have taken the pawn: 31...♗xe4 32.♗xe4 ♕xe4 33.♕e3 ♕f5∓.

32.♕b3!? ♔h8 33.♕xb4 ♕xc2 34.♖hd3!

The black bishops cannot show their strength. The loose position of the black pieces and White's extra exchange decide the assessment of the position.

34...♖d7 35.♖xd6 ♗c3 36.♕a3!

36.♕c5?? ♕xd1+ 37.♖xd1 ♖xd1+ 38.♔f2 ♗d4+.

36...♖f7 37.♖c1 ♗b2 38.♕a8+! ♗xa8 39.♖xc2 1-0

Conclusion: Do not be afraid to play original moves. Often they are strongest.

In unusual positions, normal moves rarely work. – Aron Nimzowitsch

Solution 97

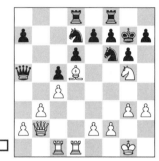

White is better. His active play in the centre and on the kingside is more important than Black's play on the queenside and along the b-file.

In the game S.Guliev-Zaitsev (Moscow 1996) there followed:

22.f4! h6 23.♘e4 ♔h7 24.♘xf6+ ♘xf6 25.♗f3 ♕c7 26.♖d2! ♖g8

Black goes over completely to defence. If he tries to organise play on the b-file, he will not be able to cope with White's kingside initiative. For example: 26...a5 27.e3 and g4-g5 etc. For positions of this type, a particularly instructive example is the classic game Keres-Szabo (Hastings 1954/55).

27.♔h2 g5 28.e3 ♖g7 29.♖g1!

And White obtained a large positional advantage.

Conclusion: In studying opening systems, it is valuable to be familiar with the games of specialists in that opening. Why reinvent the wheel?

He who forgets the past is condemned to repeat it. – Santayana

Solution 98

Black's position is better. White has problems defending the pawns on b2 and e5.

In the game Vorotnikov-S.Guliev (Moscow 1996) White tried to solve his problems in a radical way, but after

14.♗xd5? exd5 15.♕xf5 ♕xb2! 16.e6 0-0! 17.♕xd5 ♕xa1 18.♕d2 fxe6 19.♘a3 ♖ad8! 20.♕c2 ♘d4! 21.cxd4

(21.♕d3 ♕xc3!)

21...♕xd4

Black had a winning position. White should have played 14.b4! (intending the manoeuvre ♘b1-d2-b3) to fight for equality, although even here, after 14...♘fe7 or 14...♘ce7, with the threat 15...♘g6, Black's chances are superior.

Conclusion: One must be able to defend!

For success, the defender needs to be able to play combinatively better than the attacker, seeing all the critical variations and calculating them deeply! – Bent Larsen

Solution 99

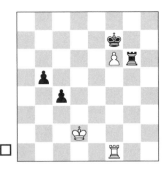

The position is drawn, although it looks bad for White. But thanks to the strong position of his rook and the discoordinated black pieces, he is able to hold.

The game S.Guliev-Zaitsev (Moscow 1996) ended as follows:

49.♖f5! b4 50.♖b5 ♖g2+ 51.♔c1 b3 52.♖b6 ♖a2 53.♖c6 ♖a4

53...♖c2+ 54.♔b1 c3 55.♖b6! ♖b2+ 56.♔c1 ♔g6 57.♖c6! – this is a position of reciprocal zugzwang.

54.♖b6 ♖a1+ 55.♔b2 ♖a2+ 56.♔b1 ♖f2 57.♖c6 ♖c2 58.♖b6 ♖f2 59.♖c6 ♖f4 60.♔b2 ♔e8 61.♔c3 ♔d7 62.♖b6 ♔e8 63.♖b7 ♔f8 64.♖c7

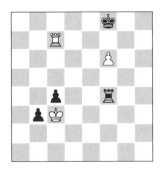

And a draw was agreed.

Conclusion: How many theoretical positions in rook endings do you remember?

A high quality of endgame technique is an unmistakeable mark of chess mastery. – Mikhail Botvinnik

Solution 100

White's pieces are very actively placed. However, he is a pawn down and his king is exposed, which may allow the opponent to gain a tempo at some point. White's queenside pawns are also weak. On the other hand, Black has not yet developed his queenside. These factors show that the game is sharp and dynamic. To assess such positions, one must be able to calculate accurately and deeply, as well as correctly judging the underlying course of the game. In the game S.Guliev-Zaitsev (Moscow 1996) White went in for the most principled variation, winning the exchange, but the strong pawn mass in the centre forces one to prefer Black's position.
15.♕f3 e5
Better was 15...♗xd4! 16.♕xa8 ♘c6 ♖xd4 ♘xd4 ♕e4 ♖e8∓.
16.♕xa8
16.♘b5 ♕c6!, but 16.♘e6 is slightly better for White: after 16...♕xe6 17.♕xa8 ♘c6, White has 18.♕b7.
16...exd4 17.♕f3 ♘c6 18.♗f6 ♗xf6
19.♕xf6 ♖e8 20.♖fe1 ♖e5 21.e4
♖a5?!=

In the initial position, White should have chosen another continuation, promising equality – this would have accorded more with the requirements of the position: **15.♕xe7 ♕xe7** (15...♖e8?! 16.♕xd7 ♘xd7 17.♘b5!) **16.♗xe7 ♖e8 17.♗a3!** (17.♗g5!?) **17...♘a6! 18.e3=**.
Also interesting is **15.♕e4**, to keep the knight protected (compared to the game, 15...♗xd4 is not attractive anymore) and with the idea to meet 15...e5 with 16.♘e6.

Conclusion: Always consider very carefully whether it is correct to disturb the balance.

The nature of the struggle in equal positions differs sharply from the dynamic change of situations that is inherent in positions with an advantage for one of the players. In such positions, the struggle, as a rule, should be conducted much more calmly. Ill-considered actions can immediately tip the scales in favour of the opponent, so the best way to fight when the forces are equal is long manoeuvring – striving to create weaknesses in the enemy position, whilst avoiding the weakening of one's own position. – Oleg Chebotarev

Solution 101

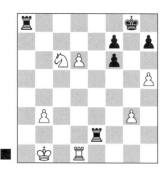

Each side has his plusses. White has an advanced, protected passed pawn, but his king is in a dangerous situation. The black rooks have good chances of organising an attack. In such positions, it is difficult to keep one's head and remain objective! As well as ability and knowledge, one also needs a strong character to take the correct decision.

In the game Drozdov-S.Guliev (Moscow 1996) Black overestimated the strength of his rooks and played:
35...♖ea2?!
After
36.♖d3! ♖a1+ 37.♔b2 ♖8a2+ 38.♔c3 ♖c1+ 39.♔b4 ♖xc6 40.d7 ♖a8 41.♔b5 ♖c1 42.d8♕+ ♖xd8 43.♖xd8+

he reached a difficult rook ending, where he eventually lost after failing to exploit all of his resources. However, if he had kept his cool, he would probably have realised that the position is equal, but that he needs to control the second rank.

By means of **35...♖aa2! 36.d7 ♖ab2+** Black gives perpetual check. The following variations show that White must also settle for this outcome:

A) 36.♖d3 ♖eb2+ 37.♔c1 ♖c2+ (37...♖g2!–+) 38.♔d1? ♖g2–+; or

B) 36.♘b4 ♖ad2 (36...♖eb2+ 37.♔c1 ♖a1+) 37.♔c1 ♖xd1+ 38.♔xd1 ♖e6 with advantage to Black, etc.

Conclusion: The miser pays twice.

The aim of all manoeuvres on open files is to penetrate to the enemy camp on the 7th or 8th ranks. – Aron Nimzowitsch

Solution 102

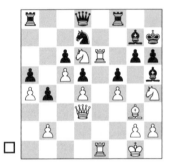

As a rule, a successfully conducted attack should end with a tactical blow. This usually lands at the most vulnerable point in the enemy position (with rare exceptions). Another important factor is the concentration of the attacking forces in that region.

Even a casual glance at the diagram position is enough to reveal that White has a large advantage and a great likelihood of a combination. In the game L.Guliev-Terekhin (St Petersburg 1997) White decided that the time had come to act!
25.♘hxf5! gxf5 26.♘xf5 ♘f6 27.♖d6 ♕b8 28.♖e7 ♖a7 29.♘xg7+ ♔g6 30.♕e2 ♖xe7 31.♕xe7 ♖f7 32.♕e3 ♘e4 33.♖xg6 ♖xg7 34.f5 ♕f8 35.♕xh6+ ♔g8 36.♗e5
And Black resigned.

Conclusion: General tasks are achieved through strategy, specific ones through tactics.

Tactics in the service of strategy. – Max Euwe

Solution 103

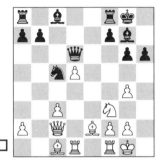

Thanks to the extra pawn and strong passed pawn on d5, the assessment is not in doubt: White has the advantage. The main things one needs to note are the weak white pawns (doubled and isolated pawns), the lack of obvious weaknesses in Black's camp and the more active position of the black pieces. These factors give Black reasonable hopes of compensation for the pawn. In the game Zakharevich-L.Guliev (St Petersburg 1997) Black even considered his position satisfactory. He hoped to be able soon to place his rooks satisfactorily and obtain good play. However, White's next move came as a great surprise:

18.♖d4!

A very strong move: the rook defends the g4-pawn, creates the threat of 19.♗f4, and also gives the game a dynamic character. Black should probably decline the 'Trojan Horse' and go for one of 18...

b6, 18...♗d7, 18...g5 etc. But at the board, he could not resist the lure of material:

18...♗xd4 19.cxd4 ♘a6 20.♘e5! ♖d8 21.♕d2! ♕f8 22.♗c4 ♘c7 23.d6 ♘e6 24.♗a3 ♕g7 25.♖e1 g5 26.♕d3 ♕f6 27.♖e3 ♕g7 28.♖f3 f6 29.d7 1-0

Conclusion: Art requires sacrifices!

In any sphere, success requires a little bit of madness. – William Shakespeare

Solution 104

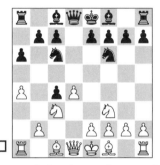

The game is in the early opening stages, and we should first of all develop the pieces.

A) However, after the direct 6.e4 Black seizes the initiative with 6...♗g4 7.d5 ♘a5!;

B) 6.d5 ♘a5! is also favourable to Black;

C) whilst after 6.e3 ♘a5 7.♘d2 ♗e6 we get a complicated game with mutual chances, Even so, White's position is superior!

In the game S.Guliev-Mirzoev (Baku 1997) White, temporarily forgetting about development, played

6.a5!

This ensures him the better chances. The game continued as follows:

129

6...♗g4 7.d5 ♘a7 8.♘e5!?

It was also worth considering 8.e4.

8...♘b5 9.♘xg4 ♘xg4 10.e4 ♘e5 11.f4 ♘d3+ 12.♗xd3 cxd3 13.♕xd3 c6 14.0-0 e6 15.♖d1

Even stronger was 15.♘xb5 axb5 16.♗e3!.

15...exd5 16.exd5 ♗c5+ 17.♔h1 0-0 18.♘e4 ♗d4 19.♘g5 g6 20.♕h3!

And White obtained a serious attack.

Conclusion: Sometimes the circumstances themselves prompt the correct decision.

The smallest fighting unit on the chessboard, the 'staunch wooden soldier', the pawn, is ready without hesitation to perform any task of the commander. – Alexander Koblencs

Solution 105

In this situation, 'playing by nose' is not sufficient. It is essential to calculate variations accurately and only then take a decision! If, after doing this, you came to the conclusion that the game is equal, you are right!

In the game S.Guliev-Yagupov (Moscow 1997) White, by means of

37.♗d5

managed to head to drawing waters. The continuation 37.f5

♗f8 or 37.♘e6 g4! 38.♘xg7 (Black threatened ...♗g7-f6-h4#) 38...♖a1 looks dangerous.

37...♖a1 38.♖d8+ ♗f8!!

38...♔h7? 39.♔xf3! g1♕ 40.♗e4#.

39.♖xf8+ ♔g7 40.♖f7+ ♔h8 41.♖f8+ ♔g7

The only move; after 41...♔h7 42.♔xf3 g1♕ 43.♗e4+ ♔g7 44.♘e6# Black again gets mated.

42.♘e6+ ♔g6 43.f5+ ♔h7

43...♔h5? 44.♗xf3+.

44.♔xf3 g1♕ 45.♖f7+ ♔g8 46.♖f8+ ♔h7 47.♖f7+

And here a draw agreement followed.

Conclusion: Risk is a noble cause.

... with correct play, one equal position leads to another. – Wilhelm Steinitz

When such adventures end in a draw, one cannot help recalling Steinitz's words. Although, if one looks at the diagram position, it is quite obvious that, during the game, each side was taking a considerable risk and did not play very accurately.

Solution 106

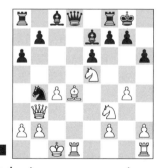

White's pieces occupy active positions, and at first glance, he has

a large advantage. But by delving into the position more deeply, one can understand that Black is better. The position of the white king is weak and if Black manages to organise an attack on the queenside, then his superiority will become clear. For this, he needs first of all to avoid the exchange of queens. With this aim, in the game Lastin-S.Guliev (Moscow 1997) Black played

19...♕e8!

After 19...♕c7?! 20.a3 ♘c6 21.♕b6! White achieves the desired exchange.

20.a3

Otherwise Black obtains a strong attack by playing ...f7-f6.

20...♘c6 21.♘xc6?!

Now the black attack develops unhindered. White should have played solidly, choosing between 21.♕b6 and 21.♗b6.

21...♕xc6 22.♘e5 ♕e8 23.f4 b5! 24.c5 ♗b7 25.♖hg1 ♗d5 26.♕c2

26...b4! 27.axb4 a5 28.bxa5 ♖xa5 29.♖g3 ♕b5! 30.♔d2 ♖d8

And Black obtained a winning attack.

Conclusion: Do you remember the methods of conducting the fight: attack, defence, manoeuvring?

Combining attack and defence is one of the precious and essential qualities of every player. Being too absorbed in one's own thoughts usually leads to an underestimation of the opponent's actions. – David Bronstein

Solution 107

Black is somewhat better. In such positions, typically arising from a King's Indian, much depends on the prospects for Black's dark-squared bishop. If it manages to secure active play or be exchanged off, then Black generally has a good game, whereas in the opposite case, he often gradually falls into a difficult position. Here, with the help of a typical manoeuvre, Black succeeds in exchanging off the bishop and create play on the kingside dark squares.

In the encounter Loginov-L.Guliev (St Petersburg 1997) Black achieved his aim as follows:

18...♗f6! 19.♔b1 ♗g5 20.♘f1 ♘c5 21.♕f2 ♗xe3 22.♕xe3 ♕f6 23.♘d2 ♕f4 24.♕e2 ♖f7 25.g3 ♕f6 26.♖h2 a4 27.♕e3 ♖af8 28.♖f1 ♖h7 29.♔a2 g5 30.♖fh1 h4 31.♕e1 ♘d3 32.♕e3 ♘c5 33.♕e1 ♘d3 34.♕e3 ♘c5 ½-½

Conclusion: How to determine the boundaries of self-belief?

Moving the pieces lightly, without going into the game deeply, I was committed to believing that the right thing would eventually prevail. – Siegbert Tarrasch

Solution 108

In the game Vaulin-L.Guliev (Smolensk 1997), the black forces are all pointing at the white king. In such situations, there is very often a decisive blow...

31...♗e3! 32.♗xe5+

Nor is he saved after 32.fxe3 ♕xg3+ or 32.♖xe3 ♖b1+ 33.♘e1 ♕h2+.

32...♘xe5

And White resigned in view of the following variations:

  A) 33.♘xe5 ♖xb3 34.♕xb3 ♕xg3+ 35.♔h1 ♕h3+ 36.♔g1 ♗xf2+;

  B) 33.♖xe3 ♘xf3+ 34.♖xf3 ♖b1+.

In this example, it is instructive that all of the black pieces were taking part in the attack as a unified group. But the most honourable place in this ensemble goes to the rook. This was the piece that destroyed the main white forces on the queenside!

Conclusion: Chess has its heroes too.

Whenever a person does something stupid, he does it out of the highest motives. – Oscar Wilde

Solution 109

White's position looks hopeless. However, it is always too early to resign. He still has some resources to put up resistance! He can enter a single-rook ending, where there are some chances of saving the game, and there are also stalemate motifs. After spotting an interesting trap, which is easy to miss in a practical game, White decided to try his last chance.

In the game L.Guliev-Shchekachev (Smolensk 1997) White played:

45.h4+!?

Black, already mentally having chalked up the point in the tournament table, did not look deeply into the position at all, and fell for the trap:

45...♔g4??

And White was twice able to exploit the motif of the 'desperado rook', to set up a stalemate:

46.♖g6+ ♔h3 47.♖f3+!!

And the players agreed a draw, because of the following variations:

  A) 47...exf3 48.♖g3+ ♔xh4 49.♖g4+ ♔h3 50.♖g3+;

  B) 47...♔xh4 48.♖h3+ ♔xh3 49.♖g3+ ♔h4 50.♖g4+.

Correct was **45...♔xh4! 46.♖xf5 ♖h2+**, and Black retains every chance of winning the game.

Conclusion: One must fight to the very end!

Try every possibility. It is always important to know that you have done everything possible. – Charles Dickens

Solution 110

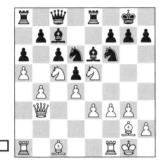

White is better. His active knights and the possibility of beginning a pawn storm on the kingside determine his advantage. By means of **21.g4!** White could have started a strong attack. It is not easy for Black to find a satisfactory regrouping of his minor pieces. However, in the game S.Guliev-Timman (Pula 1997) White chose
21.♕d1?
and after the moves
21...♗h3 22.♖a2 ♗xg2 23.♖xg2 ♘f5
the game became sharper. There followed:
24.f4?
White should probably have gone for 24.g4 ♘h4 25.♖e2 with sharp play.
24...♘d6 25.g4
White finally plays this move, but it's rather late.
25...♘fe4
And Black had no problems at all. Having missed the chance to play 21.g4! at the right time, White played it in an inferior form!

Conclusion: Active moves played at the wrong time are like over-ripe fruit.

Everything at its right time. (proverb)

Solution 111

If you suggested 6.♗d3?, then you fell for a trap and lost: 6...♘xc3 7.♕d2 cxd4 8.exd4 e5!! 9.♗xe5 ♗b4. In the game S.Guliev-Vaisser (Pula 1997), White, having seen this hidden trap, played
6.♘e2!
and after the moves
6...d5?!
(more solid was 6...cxd4 7.exd4 d5)
7.dxc5! e6 8.a3!
obtained the better game. As the saying goes, do not dig a pit for someone else, because you might fall into it yourself. In life generally, this is bad and can be very dangerous, although in chess, there is sometimes value in falling into trouble, so as to acquire experience of defending difficult positions.

Conclusion: After the opponent has made his move, it is useful to ask yourself: what does he want?

He who expects too much from the opening gets nothing. – Hans Kmoch

Solution 112

White has a decisive advantage. However, if he is cowardly and retreats the bishop, then after 13.♗d3 f5!, and then ...g7-g6 and ...♗g7, Black will be able to consolidate his position.
Therefore in the game S.Guliev-Vaisser (Pula 1997) White, after long thought, decided on the sharp continuation
13.0-0-0
after which White's attack is hardly to be resisted.
However, **13.♕e5!** was even stronger, for example: 13...♕d6 14.♘xd5+ ♚d8 15.♕g5+ f6 16.♘xf6 h6 17.♕h4+–.
There followed
13...axb5 14.♕e5 f6
(14...♖a8 15.♘xd5+ ♚e8 16.♘c7+)
15.♕xb8
and White obtained a winning position.
  A) We should note that, in the event of 13...♕c7 14.♖xd5 axb5 15.♘xb5 ♕c6 (after 15...♕a5 16.♖d3, with the threats 17.♕c5 and 17.♖hd1, or 15...♕b6 16.♖d6 ♕a5 17.♖hd1, White's advantage is not in doubt) 16.♖c5 ♕xg2 17.♖d1 ♕xf2 18.♕e5 the black position is very difficult;
  B) If 13...f5, then 14.e4! axb5 15.exf5 is very strong for White.

Conclusion: If the enemy king is trapped in the centre and unable to castle, then attack it decisively, not being afraid of sacrifices!

... the ability to play combinations, to find in any position the most purposeful move, leading most quickly to the fulfilment of the plan, is above all principles – more than that, it is the ONLY principle in chess, that is capable of definition. – Mikhail Chigorin

Solution 113

Certainly, the position is very complicated. Black, with the exception of the 'hole' on d6, has a position with no weaknesses and a healthy pawn structure. White has two bishops and good development. The next few moves should determine the picture of the game. If Black manages to establish a blockade on the e5-square (for example with ...f7-f6 and ...♘e5), his position will be better.
In the game Kengis-S.Guliev (Pula 1997) Black thought about all this for a long time and eventually even fell into time trouble. A significant role in this was played by the next choice of move.
There followed:
21...0-0-0

A) In the event of 21...♗h3 22.♗xh3 ♖xh3 23.e5! ♘c5 24.♔g2! (24.♗e3! ♘e6?! 25.♗xb6 axb6 26.♘e4 with attack) 24...♖h8 25.b4 ♘e6 26.♘e4! White's advantage is not in doubt;

B) Also after 21...♘c4 22.e5 ♘xb2 23.♖b1 ♘c4 24.♖xb7 ♘cxe5 25.♖e1 f6 26.♗xe5 fxe5 (26...♘xe5 27.♖xg7!) 27.♗xc6 Black's position is difficult;

C) He is also under pressure after 21...f6 22.e5 f5 23.♗g5! (also interesting is 23.♖e3!? with the idea of transferring the rook to g3);

D) Only the sensible **21...0-0** allows Black to retain equality, e.g. 22.e5 ♘d5 (22...♖fe8!?) 23.♘xd5 cxd5!, and Black is perfectly all right.
22.e5 ♘c5?!
More solid was 22...♘d5! 23.♘xd5 cxd5, although here too, after 24.♖e3! ♔b8 25.♖g3 White's pressure is obvious.
23.b4?!
23.♗e3!±.
23...♘ca4 24.♖e3? ♘xc3 25.♖xc3

And now instead of 25...♘d7? 26.b5!, after which White's advantage assumed real proportions, Black could have got the better chances after 25...♖d4 26.a3 ♘d5 27.♗xd5 ♗xd5+ 28.♔g1 ♖h4 29.♗g3 ♖he4.

Conclusion: By studying one's own games, one can learn many wise lessons!

Always play honestly, if you have all the trumps in your hand. – Oscar Wilde

Solution 114

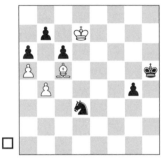

White's position is hopeless. His counterplay is insufficient to make a draw. However, by stubborn resistance, he can force his opponent to be extremely accurate. This can be achieved as follows:
68.♗d6! ♔h4 69.♔c7 g3 70.♔xb7 (70.♗xg3+ ♔xg3 71.♔xb7 ♘xb4 72.♔b6 ♔f4 73.♔c5 ♔e5 74.♔xb4 ♔d4-+) **70...g2 71.♗h2 ♘xb4 72.♔b6 ♔h3 73.♗g1 ♔g3 74.♔c5 ♘d3+ 75.♔xc6!** (75.♔b6 ♘f2 76.♔xa6 ♘h3 77.♔b7 ♘xg1 78.a6 ♘f3 79.a7 g1♕ 80.a8♕ ♕b1+! 81.♔c7 ♕h7+ 82.♔b6 ♘e5-+) **75...♘f2 76.♔b6 ♘h3 77.♔xa6! ♘xg1 78.♔b7 ♘f3 79.a6 g1♕ 80.a7!.**

analysis diagram

As we see, an unusual position is reached almost by force. Black has queen and knight, and White has a strong pawn on a7. I finished my analysis here and for a long time considered the position drawn. When I was trainer of the Turkish team, I once showed my analysis to IM Atakishi, and he found a surprising way to win for Black. It involves allowing the a7-pawn to promote. The win is as follows: 80...♛b1+ 81.♚a6 ♛d3+ 82.♚b7 ♛d7+ 83.♚b8 ♞e5−+.

But the game S.Guliev-Timman (Pula 1997) continued:

68.♗g1? ♞xb4 69.♚c7 g3 70.♚xb7 ♚g4 71.♚b6 ♚f3 72.♚c5 ♚g2 73.♗d4 ♞d3+ 74.♚xc6

74.♚b6 c5! 75.♚xa6 cxd4 76.♚b5 ♚f2 77.a6 g2 78.a7 g1♛ 79.a8♛ ♛c1−+.

74...♚f1 75.♚b6 g2

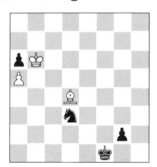

Black is ready to play 76...♞f2, after which White lacks one tempo to achieve a theoretically drawn position, and so he resigned.

In my first analysis after the game, written out in 1997, I believed the most tenacious continuation to be 68.♗a7?! g3 69.♚c7 g2 70.♗g1 (70.♚xb7 c5!) 70...♚g4 71.♚xb7 ♞xb4 72.♚b6 ♚f3 73.♚c5 ♞d3+ 74.♚xc6! ♚e2 75.♚b6 ♚f1 76.♗h2 ♞f2 77.♚xa6 ♞g4 78.♚b7 ♞xh2 79.a6 g1♛ 80.a7.

But in 2003, whilst browsing through my old notebook, I found mistakes in my analysis. Black can easily refute these white tries, in two different ways:

A) 68...♞xb4 69.♚c7 ♞d3 70.♚xb7 c5! 71.♚xa6 g3! (71...c4 72.♗d4) 72.♗b8 g2 73.♗h2 c4 74.♚b5 (74.♚b7 c3 75.a6 ♞c5+) 74...c3 75.a6 c2 76.a7 c1♛ 77.a8♛ ♛c5+ 78.♚a6 ♛a3+ 79.♚b7 ♛xa8+ 80.♚xa8 ♞e1! 81.♗g1 ♚g4 82.♚b7 ♚f3 83.♚c6 ♚e2 84.♚d5 ♚f1 85.♗a7 ♞d3 and ...♞f2−+;

B) The second path is even more convincing: 68...g3 69.♚c7 c5! 70.bxc5 ♞e5! 71.♚xb7 ♞c6−+.

Conclusion: From time to time, it can be useful to revisit your old analyses.

I do not understand evil-doing. If you want to annoy someone, it is enough to tell the truth about them. – Friedrich Nietzsche

Solution 115

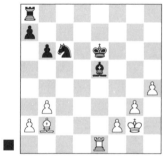

A very complicated position. White has three passed pawns against a piece.

Since the white pawns are not very far advanced, they are not very dangerous. Black faces a difficult choice. The move 35...♔f5?? is bad because of 36.g4+! ♔f4 37.f3! and there is no defence against 38.♖e4 mate.

In the game Akopian-S.Guliev (Pula 1997) Black, who was in time trouble, saw this and quickly played

35...♔f6?!

missing

36.♖xe5! ♘xe5 37.f4

Surprisingly, here the chances of the two sides are still roughly equal! There followed

37...♔f5! 38.♗xe5 ♔g4 39.h5!

(otherwise Black can seize the initiative with the manoeuvre ...♖a8-c8-c2)

39...♖c8?? 40.h6 ♖c2+ 41.♔g1 ♖c1+ 42.♔f2 ♖h1 43.♗g7 ♔f5 44.♔g2 ♖h5 45.♔f3 ♖h3 46.♗f8 b5?! 47.b4 a6 48.♗g7 ♔g6 49.♔g2 ♖h5 50.g4 ♖h4 51.♔f3 ♖h2 52.f5+ ♔g5 53.♔e4

and Black resigned.

However, by keeping his cool Black could have defended successfully with 39...♔xh5!, e.g. 40.♔f3 ♖c8 (also good is 40...♖e8 or 40...♖g8) 41.g4+ ♔g6 42.♔e4 ♖c2 with roughly equal chances.

The position in the diagram is also equal. It was just necessary to spot all the traps and play **35...♔d5!**. Black overlooked 36.♖xe5 and then, in shock, missed 39...♔xh5 as

well. As we see, the old saying that misfortunes rarely come in singles is true in chess as well!

The height of power is power over your own thinking. – Winston Churchill

Solution 116

White is winning. However, the position remains complicated. It is essential to be brave and purposeful and play sharply! **1.♘e7+! ♔h8 2.g4!** and Black has no satisfactory defence against the threat of 3.g5!. For example:

A) 2...♗d2 3.♕c5! ♗e1+ 4.♔e3 – the ♗c4 is attacked and 4.♘xg6+ threatened;

B) 2...♖fa8 3.g5 ♗f8 4.♕c5 (also good is 4.h4). Black has a very difficult, scarcely defensible, position.

If you did not find this variation, do not despair, because in the game S.Guliev-Korotylev (Moscow 1997) White also missed this chance and played:

1.♘xb4? ♖d8 2.♘d5 ♖c1?

After 2...♗xd5 3.exd5 ♗f8!, despite the two-pawn deficit, the initiative passes to Black and his position is already preferable.

3.♘e7+ ♔h8 4.g4!?

White finds this idea a little late, and here Black has an original way to save himself:

4...♗d2!!

4...♖d2+? 5.♔g3!+−.

5.♕c7 ♗e1+ 6.♔e3 ♗d2+

And White cannot avoid perpetual check.

Conclusion: In the attack, one should not worry about trifling amounts of material, but should as a priority try to realise the main idea.

The aesthetics of chess are for me primarily the correctness of the idea, its truth, revealed in the clear logic of thought. – Vasily Smyslov

Solution 117

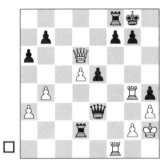

It is well known that then Soviet theorist Peter Romanovsky described major-piece endings as the fourth stage of a game of chess. As a rule in such positions, the attack on the king is one of the defining features. Unlike his opponent's, all of White's forces are pointed at the enemy king. This fact is of decisive significance here. White is winning. Before the final assault, he must activate his last piece.
In the game L.Guliev-Zhelnin (Kaluga 1997) White played

1.♖f5!

(but not 1.♕f6?? ♕g3+) and after

1...♖d1 2.♖xg7+ ♔xg7 3.♕f6+

Black resigned.
As the following variations show, White's attack is irresistible even after other black first moves:

A) 1...♖d4 2.♖xg7+ ♔xg7 3.♕f6+ ♔g8 4.♖g5+;

B) 1...f6 (the most tenacious) 2.♕e6+ ♖f7 3.♖xh4, and the only defence against the threat of 4.♕e8+ ♖f8 5.♖h8+ ♔xh8 6.♕xf8+ ♔h7 7.♖h5+ ♔g6 8.♕e8, mating, is 3...♕e2, but here too, after 4.♖g4 there is no stopping 5.♖h5 and 6.♕e8+.

Conclusion: In major-piece endings, a weak king is a very important factor.

The proper tone must be kept, Else your wishes won't be met! – M.Akhbeli

Solution 118

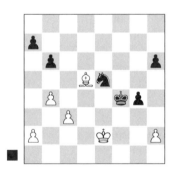

Endgame experts, who know how to take the initiative, will not be confused. Black is winning. In the game Dovliatov-S.Guliev (Baku 1998) Black first crippled White's pawn majority on the queenside.

49...b5

His further plans involve the advance of the pawns on the kingside. The game continued:
50.♗b7 h5 51.♗a6 h4 52.♗xb5 h3!
The key move of Black's idea. Although White has won a pawn, in the meantime the black kingside pawns have advanced too far and cannot be stopped.
53.c4 ♘f3! 54.♗d7
54.c5 ♘d4+ and then ♘xb5–+.
54...♘xh2 55.c5 ♘f3 56.♔f1
56.c6 h2 57.c7 h1♕ 58.c8♕ ♕e1+ 59.♔d3 ♕d2+ 60.♔c4 ♕xd7 61.♕xd7 ♘e5+.
56...♔g3 57.♗xg4 h2 0-1

Conclusion: In the endgame, with pawns on both flanks, a bishop is not always superior to a knight.

The best mountains can only be ones I have never been on. – Vladimir Vysotsky

Solution 119

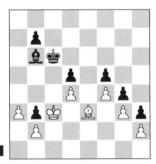

White will win the b3-pawn. Naturally, this promises him some chances. However, the unfortunate pawn structure, hampering his bishop, prevents him counting on the victory. The game is equal. In the game Gadzhili-S.Guliev (Baku 1998), after the following moves, the players realised that neither of them could strengthen his position and so a draw was agreed.
59...♗a5+ 60.♔xb3 ♗e1 61.♗g1
The only move; the threat was 63...♗xg3!.
61...♔b5 62.♔c2 ♔a4 63.♔d1 ♗a5 64.♔c2 ♗e1 65.♔d1 ♗a5 66.♔c2
½-½
As we know, one of Capablanca's golden rules was:

When the opponent has a bishop, you should usually try to place your pawns on the same colour squares as this bishop. On the other hand, if you have a bishop, then regardless of whether or not the opponent also has one, place your pawns on the opposite colour squares as those on which your bishop stands.

However, I don't think it is superfluous to point out that the original author of this rule was the French master Philidor, who in his book *Analysis of the Game of Chess* (published in 1749) wrote:

If my bishop controls the light squares, I should place my pawns on dark squares: in this case, my bishop can attack the enemy pieces which tried to hide amongst the pawns.

As we see, it is precisely this factor that prevents White getting the benefits of his extra pawn.

Conclusion: Rules are made to be observed.

Do not despise advice before examining it. – Ivan Krylov

Solution 120

For a reader with sharp combinative vision, who has already solved many simple combinations, this example will be easy.
White can end the game with a pretty combination. He has a decisive advantage.

34.♖c8+!

This nice move was the last in the game Sowray-S.Guliev (Berlin 1998).

Conclusion: The rook is the only piece which controls the same number of squares, regardless of whether it stands in the centre of the board or on the edge.

The rook must wait until its path is cleared, before it can invade the enemy camp. – Alexander Koblencs

Solution 121

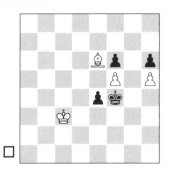

White wins: **64.♔d4! e3 65.♗c4 ♔xf5 66.♔d5! ♔f4** (66...♔g5 67.♗e2 f5 68.♔e6!) **67.♗e2 ♔f5 68.♗d1! ♔f4 69.♔e6! f5**

analysis diagram

70.♔d5! (70.♔f6? ♔e4 71.♔g6 f4 72.♔xh6 f3 72.♗xf3+=) **70...♔g3** (70...♔g5 71.♔e5 f4 72.♗f3!+−) **71.♔e5 f4 72.♔e4! ♔f2 73.♔xf4 e2 74.♗xe2 ♔xe2 75.♔f5** and White is one tempo too fast for his opponent. Anyone who found this has splendid endgame technique and mastery in calculating variations.
In the game S.Guliev-Al-Sayed (Elista 1998) White saw this variation at the board, but it seemed too complicated (after all, everything hangs on one tempo!). Worrying about miscalculating, White did not go in for it. It seemed to him that

64.♔d2

also led to a win and was more solid and careful. However, later he realised that he had committed a serious mistake. The game continued as follows:

64...♔f3 65.♔e1?!

After this, Black gets the chance to further muddy the waters. The e3-square plays an important role and control of it should not be relinquished. More to the point was the waiting move 65.♗d7! or 65.♗c8. In the latter case, after 65...e3 66.♔e1 we reach a position which occurred in the game (to which we will return). Therefore, let us look at the first continuation: 65.♗d7 ♔f2 66.♗b5! ♔f3 (66...e3+ 67.♔d1 ♔f3 68.♔e1 etc.) 67.♗c6! ♔f4 68.♗d7 ♔f3 69.♔c3 ♔f4 70.♔d4 e3 71.♗b5 ♔xf5 72.♔d5! – as we can easily see, the game has transposed into the variation we examined above.

65...e3?!

After this, White's task is greatly simplified. By means of 65...♔e3! Black could have posed his opponent serious problems. However, deep analysis shows that even then, White can return to the winning variation that we showed at the very start of this section. For example: 65...♔e3 66.♗d7 ♔f3 (66...♔d3 67.♔f2) 67.♔d2!.

66.♗d7

68...e2

This also eases White's task. More tenacious resistance could have been offered, with the possibility that the opponent will go wrong!: 66...♔f4 67.♔e2 ♔e4 68.♗c8 ♔f4 69.♔d3! ♔f3 70.♗a6!! ♔f4 (70...e2 71.♔d2 ♔f4 72.♗d3!) 71.♔d4! ♔xf5 72.♔d5! ♔f4 73.♗e2 ♔g3 74.♔e4? ♔f2 75.♗d1 e2 76.♗xe2 ♔xe2 77.♔f5

♔e3 78.♔xf6 (78.♔g6 f5 79.♔xf5 ♔d4) 78...♔e4 79.♔g6 ♔e5 80.♔xh6 ♔f6 and a draw.

However, with 74.♔e6! White could still return to the variation we want. **67.♗a4! ♔e4 68.♗c2+ ♔e3 69.♗b1! ♔f3 70.♗d3 ♔e3 71.♗xe2 ♔e4 72.♗g4 ♔f4 73.♗h3 ♔g5 74.♔f2 ♔f4 75.♔g2 ♔e4 76.♔g3 ♔e3 77.♔g2 ♔e2 78.♔f4 ♔f2 79.♗f3 ♔g1 80.♔e4 ♔f2**

And now Black resigned without waiting for the reply.

Conclusion: Why go round the sun to get to the moon?

It is not for nothing that the great players of the past devoted considerable attention to the endgame. In learning the secrets of mastery, I realised that the approach to the heights of chess art lies via a knowledge of the laws of the endgame. – Vasily Smyslov

Solution 122

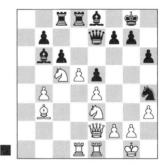

The game is equal. White has a space advantage, but he should not succeed in exploiting this advantage. The connections between his front and rear lines are not sufficient! White will not be able to strengthen c5 and d5. Here we recall the military principle that the space and connections between the front line and the rear must be exactly right, not more and not less. By means of **29...♗xc5 30.bxc5 cxd5!** Black could break up the position and maintain the balance. In this case, after 31.♕g4 ♔h7 32.g3 ♘g6 33.♘f5 the chances are roughly equal. In the game S.Guliev-Ghorbani (Elista 1998), after the moves **29...♗xc5 30.bxc5**

Black momentarily lost his cool and played

30...♕xc5?

and after

31.d6!

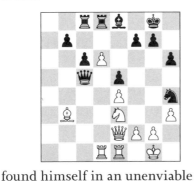

found himself in an unenviable position. There followed

31...♕b4

(31...♖xd6 32.♖xd6 ♕xd6 33.♕g4! and Black loses a piece)

32.♕g4 ♕xb3 33.♕xh4 ♗d7 34.♖b1 ♕e6 35.♖xb7 ♕xd6 36.♖d1 ♕e6 37.♘f5 g5 38.♕h5 ♗e8 39.♘xh6+ ♔f8 40.♖xd8 ♖xd8 41.♕xg5

and White achieved a winning position.

Conclusion: When was the last time you overlooked a zwischenzug?

The ruling factor is space. – Alexey Suetin

Solution 123

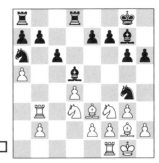

Accurate calculation of variations shows that it is possible to take the pawn and that this leads to an advantage for White.

In the game S.Guliev-Kazhgaleyev (Elista 1998), White, by means of

19.♖xb7! c5 20.♘fe5!

(the key move)

20...♘xe5 21.dxe5 c4!? 22.♘f4 ♗xg2 23.♔xg2 ♗xe5 24.♖c1 g5 25.♘h5

etc. obtained a large advantage.

Conclusion: The opponent should not be taken at his word!

Avoid those who try to break your faith in the opportunity to achieve something significant in life. This feature is peculiar to small souls. – Mark Twain

Solution 124

The position is extremely complicated and every move can

shift the balance in favour of one side or the other. In such situations, accurate calculation of variations usually comes to our aid.

A) In the event of 25.♗d5? ♖a5! 26.e4 ♗xe4+ 27.♔h2 ♖xd5 Black wins;

B) But after the continuation 25.♖f1 g6 (the only move; 25...♗h7? 26.♘d7) 26.e4 ♖a5! 27.♘c4! (27.exf5? ♖xe5 28.fxg6 ♔g7 favours Black) 27...♖c5 28.exf5 ♖xc4 29.fxg6 ♔g7 30.♗xb7 ♔xg6 31.♗d5 ♖c5 32.♗b3 White is better, but it is not obvious how he can realise his advantage. As Morozevich wrote in his analysis (*Shakhmaty v SSSR* Nr 4/1998, p.45), he calculated this continuation at the board. As can be seen, the main idea of Black's defence is based on the manoeuvre ...♖a8-a5.

Therefore, in the game S.Guliev-Morozevich (Moscow 1998) White began by depriving the enemy rook of access to the desired square.

25.b4! ♖a3
Black threatens 26...♖e3, driving the knight from the e5-square. He also blockades the a-pawn in the process.

26.e4!
26.g4 ♖e3 27.♘c4 ♖c3 28.♘e5 ♖e3 or 26.♖f1 g6 27.e4 ♖e3 28.exf5 ♖xe5 29.fxg6 ♖e6 30.♗xb7 ♖xg6 31.♖f3 does not give White anything serious.

26...♖e3 27.g4!
Here too, after 27.♖f1 g6 28.g4 ♗xe4 29.♗xe4 ♖xe4 30.♘xg6+ the position is probably drawn.

27...♗h7
27...♗xe4 28.♗xe4 ♖xe4 29.♘g6+ or 27...♖xe4 28.♗xe4 ♗xe4+ 29.♔g1 g5 30.♖e1 ♗h7 31.♖d1 ♔g7 32.♖d6 also does not save Black.

28.♖f1
Better was 28.g5 hxg5 29.♖f1 g6 30.♘d7+–.

28...g5 29.♘d7 ♔g7 30.♘xf8 ♔xf8 31.♖f6 b5?
31...♗xe4 32.♗xe4 ♖xe4 33.♖xb6 ♖xg4 34.♖xb7 h5=.

32.♔g1! ♖g3
32...♗xe4 33.♔f2.

33.e5
And in view of the variation 33...♗e4 34.e6! ♖xg2+ 35.♔f1 etc. Black resigned.

Conclusion: How many more squares does a centrally-placed knight control, than one on the edge of the board?

Secure outposts for knights and bishops in the centre are of serious importance. – Mikhail Botvinnik

Solution 125

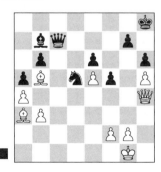

In the game S.Guliev-Vaulin (Moscow 1998) White decided that Black could not take the pawn because of the mating threats and so he played ♗c1-a3. However, Black did not believe his opponent. He played:

39...♕xe5! 40.♕d8+ ♔h7 41.♗e8 ♘f4 42.♗f7 ♘h3+!

and because of the unavoidable mate (43.♔f1 ♗a6+; 43.gxh3 ♕e1+ 44.♔h2 ♕xf2#; 43.♔h1 ♕e1+ 44.♔h2 ♕g1+ etc.) White resigned.

Conclusion: If three enemy pieces are simultaneously pointing at one king, such attacks almost always end successfully.

Measure seven times, cut once.
(proverb)

Solution 126

Certainly it is not easy to defend against the white pieces massed on the kingside. His attack is dangerous and White stands better. In the game Belikov-S.Guliev (Moscow 1998) Black thought for a long time and decided that the only way to put up tenacious resistance was with an exchange sacrifice, after which he can try to organise play on the dark squares and exploit the distance of the white pieces from the centre.

The game continued:

17...♖xc1+ 18.♖xc1 ♖e8 19.♖e1 ♕a5 20.♔f1 ♕xa2

And now White, seeing that Black had obtained strong counterplay, sought a way to equalise. After

21.♖h3 ♕xb2 22.♕xh7+ ♔f8 23.♖f3 ♕xd4 24.♗xg6! fxg6 25.♕h8+ ♔f7

(25...♔e7? 26.♖xe6+!)

26.♕h7+ ♔f8 27.♕h8+ ♔f7 28.♕h7+

the game ended in a draw by perpetual check.

In lengthy joint analysis after the game, it turned out that White did have the advantage after all, which he could have strengthened by means of 20.♕xh7+ ♔f8 21.♖he5!.

Conclusion: It is often useful in defence to sacrifice material to sharpen the position.

Sometimes, stop and look back, otherwise you'll forget where you came from and where you're going! – Alexander Belyaev

Solution 127

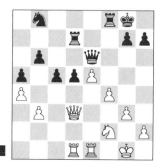

White has a large pawn majority on the kingside and Black on the queenside. But after a more attentive

look at the position, we see that the white king is somewhat weakened. In addition, his kingside pawns are stopped and it is not obvious how they can be set in motion in the near future. Black's position is better.

If it were White's move, he would probably play h2-h4, so as to support his kingside chain. But it is Black to play, and in the game Kulikov-S. Guliev (Moscow 1998) he landed an unexpected counterblow:

29...g5!

And it transpired that White had problems. There followed

30.fxg5 ♘c6 31.♕e3

(31.♘e4 ♘xe5 32.♘f6+ ♕xf6!)

31...♖df7 32.♘d3 ♖f3 33.♕d2 ♘d4 34.♖f1 ♖xf1+ 35.♖xf1 ♘f3+ 36.♖xf3 ♖xf3 37.♔g2 ♖f5

and White's position became hopeless.

In his book *Think Like a Grandmaster*, Kotov correctly writes:

Never advance pawns on the side where you stand worse.

The same thought is expressed by Capablanca in *Chess Fundamentals* in this way:

Pawns on the second rank are an advantage for the defence and a hindrance for the attack.

As we have just seen, this rule, like all rules in chess, has its exceptions. Can there be rules without exceptions?

Conclusion: One should also pay attention to the exceptions to the rules.

Solution 128

The game is still in the opening stages, but Black already has some questions to answer. If you suggested the moves **5...d5** or **5... d6**, then you have a good sense of danger. But if you decided to play 5...0-0?, then you need to work in this area, as your instinct for self-preservation is not on the requisite level!

In the game S.Guliev-Nikolaev (St Petersburg 1998) Black played

5...0-0?

and after

6.h4! h5?!

(6...d5 7.h5 is also dangerous)

7.g4! hxg4 8.♕xg4 d5 9.♕g2 ♕d6 10.h5! f5 11.♘c3 c6 12.0-0-0

he fell under a very strong attack. It is well known that the first stage of a chess game is seizing the centre, the second the development of the pieces, and the third castling, to secure the king, etc. Then the game goes into the middlegame stage and the player must assess the position. On the basis of this assessment, he forms a strategic plan and begins to fight for its fulfilment.

The example above shows what sad consequences can follow from failing to observe these postulates!

An aphorism is almost the best form in which to express a philosophical judgement. – Lev Tolstoy

Solution 129

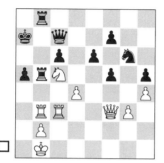

Although Black has two extra pawns, the insecure position of his king and the offside knight give White a dynamic advantage. In the game L.Guliev-Radjabov (Baku 1998) Black momentarily forgot about the knight's leaping ability. After the forced
36.♘a6! ♕b7 37.♘xb8 ♔xb8 38.♖xb5 cxb5 39.♕d3 ♔a7
White had a decisive advantage. The black king is forced to worry about his safety himself. But the broken black position does not allow him to find a safe refuge. Going into the endgame with 39...♕e4 40.♕xe4 fxe4 41.♖c5 also fails to solve the problems. There followed:
40.♖c5 ♔a6 41.d5 ♘e5 42.♕d4 ♘d7 43.♖c6+ ♘b6 44.♕c5 exd5 45.♖h6 b4 46.♖xh5 d4 47.♖h6 d3 48.♖c6! ♕b8 49.♕xf5 ♕d8
49...d2 50.♕d3+ ♔b7 51.♖d6.
50.♕f6 ♕b8 51.♕d6 ♕b7 52.♕xd3+ ♔a7 53.♕b5 1-0
In this game we saw how the black queen was weak in defence, whilst the white queen was strong in attack.

Conclusion: Strong pieces often feel out of place in defence.

Imagination is more important than knowledge. – Albert Einstein

Solution 130

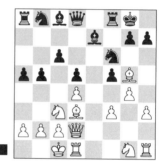

The position is very sharp and complicated. If you consider that Black is better, then with opposite-side castling, in organising an attack on the king, one must not forget about the centre. And if you suggested the move
1...♖a7!
then this shows that you have a good feeling for dynamic harmony among the pieces.
In the game Volkov-S.Guliev (Karaganda 1999), after the moves
2.♘ge2
(2.gxf5 ♘h5 3.♗xe7 ♖xe7 4.♕g5 ♕e8!)
2...♘e4! 3.♗xe7 ♖xe7
Black seized the initiative.

Conclusion: Do not forget about 'reserve' routes, when developing the pieces.

Directness does not always promise the quickest way to the aim. – S.Letz

Solution 131

In the game Babaev-L.Guliev (Baku 1999) the serious weakening of the white king allowed Black to land a decisive tactical blow, without any regrouping of his forces:
1...♗f2! 2.♔g2 e3+ 3.♔f1 ♕d6 4.♘xf7 ♖xf7 5.♗xf7+ ♔xf7 6.♖xa4 ♖xa4 7.♖xa4 ♕c6 8.g6+ hxg6 9.fxg6+ ♔e7! 0-1

Conclusion: Make way for the bishop!

He who has the bishops has the future. – Siegbert Tarrasch

Solution 132

Black should have played **1...♗e6**, preparing ...♘f6-d7, or **1...♕b6= 2.♗a3 a5 3.♗xb4 axb4**.
But in the game Malaniuk-S.Guliev (Karaganda, 1999) Black effectively shut his eyes and played

1...♖c2
and after
2.♗a3 ♖fc8??
(2...♖cc8 3.♕d2 a5 4.♖fc1 ♕b6±)
3.♗c4!
was forced to resign! After the game, one of the authors of the present book asked his experienced grandmaster opponent what he should do to avoid such oversights. Vladimir advised writing down the move on the scoresheet before playing it, then once again checking one's calculations, and only then making the move on the board. I started following this wise advice, and it seemed to help, as the number of blunders was reduced, although, alas, not eliminated entirely.
But recently FIDE changed the rules, and it is now forbidden to write down one's move before playing it. Now I do not know what to advise young players to avoid blunders.

Conclusion: Win, loss, draw – these are just the result of the battle.

The player should have self-control and not throw the board in the air when he loses. – Romain Rolland

Solution 133

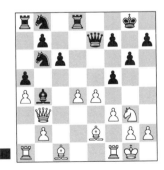

White has two bishops and a clear superiority in the centre. Black needs to do something urgently. After 1...fxe4? 2.fxe4 ♖xd4 3.♗e3 ♗c5 4.♗xd4 ♗xd4+ 5.♔h1 the opening of the f-file makes White's position preferable. After quiet development with 1...♘a6 2.♗e3, again the white trumps are likely soon to be felt.

In view of this, in the game Vladimirov-S.Guliev (Karaganda 1999) Black decided to sacrifice the exchange to complicate the game:
1...♖xd4!

He is counting on the following variation: 2.♗e3 ♗c5 3.♗xd4 (3.♕c3? ♖d5! with advantage to Black. In the post-mortem, Evgeny admitted that in his preliminary calculations, he had missed this move) 3...♗xd4+ 4.♔h1 f4 5.♖fd1! ♗f2 6.♘f1 ♘8d7, and a very interesting situation arises: although White has an extra exchange, thanks to his strong play on the dark squares, Black's position must be preferred.

Squares of a certain colour can have their own internal life and their fate influences the other colour squares too. – Alexander Alekhine

At the board, after long thought, White declined the sacrifice. With the idea of organising an attack on the king, he played:
2.exf5!?
However, after the following moves, Black obtained a large advantage.
2...♘8d7 3.f4 ♖f8 4.fxg6 hxg6 5.f5 ♖h4!

There is already a threat of 6...♗c5+ 7.♔h1 ♖xh2+!.
6.h3 ♘d5 7.fxg6 fxg6 8.♗f3 ♕e5 9.♕d3 ♔g7 10.♗d1 ♖d4
etc.

Conclusion: Complications should not always be avoided!

Solution 134

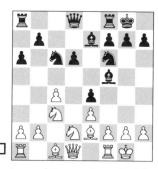

There is nothing to be afraid of, the pawn can be taken.
In the game S.Guliev-Scherbakov (Petropavlovsk 1999) after the moves
1.g4! ♗g6 2.g5 ♘e8 3.♘dxe4 f5!?
(3...♗xg5?! 4.f4 ♗xe4 5.♘xe4 ♗h4 6.♗f3±)
4.gxf6 ♘xf6 5.♘g3 ♕c8 6.f4! ♔h8 7.♗d3
(7.b3!?±) White had not only an extra pawn, but also the better position.

Conclusion: To believe or disbelieve the opponent, one should have objective reasons!

Courage is the first step to victory. – Plutarch

Solution 135

If you decided that Black's compensation is sufficient, then you have a good feel for the initiative. Interesting is **1...♞xg4**. As is clear from the variations 2.♕xg4 ♕xb7 3.c6 ♕e7, Black has rich play for the pawn, thanks to his numerous threats. For example: ...♖d8-d5-g5, ...♖c8 or ...♗d6 etc. However, in the game Filippov-S. Guliev (Petropavlovsk 1999) Black chose
1...♗xc5
and White, with the aid of a beautiful combination, returned the material and seized the initiative. There followed
2.b4! ♗xb4
(2...♗d6!?)
3.a5! ♕e5
(A) 3...♞xg4? 4.♕xg4 ♕xb7 5.♖b1 ♖b8 6.♗d2+–;
  B) Better was 3...♗d6 4.♖b1 ♗c7 5.♔g2 ♗xa5 6.♖h1 ♖b8 7.♗a3 ♕xa3 8.♕xf6 ♕c3 9.♕f3 ♕e5=)
4.♖a4

etc.
Over the board, Black underestimated the strength of 3.a5!.

Conclusion: A strong will is no mean thing.

Correct behaviour suffers more from weak will than lack of knowledge. – Herbert Spencer

Solution 136

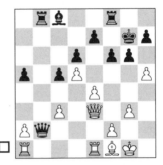

On the queenside, Black's position is better, but White has a space advantage in the centre and on the kingside. After all, he can organise an attack (e.g. with f2-f4, e4-e5). Meanwhile, it is hard for Black to make anything serious out of his advantage on the queenside. The position is equal, but easier to play for White.
In the game S.Guliev-Shchekachev (Petropavlovsk 1999) White played:
1.h6+!
Firstly it is useful to make the black king position even more vulnerable, at the same time stabilising the situation on the flank and planning to shift the weight of the struggle to the centre, by preparing f2-f4 and e4-e5.
1...♔g8 2.♗e2

Before carrying out the pawn break, White frees the f-file, so that, if necessary, he can seize it at once.

2...♗d7 3.f4 ♕a3

Black has achieved nothing by bringing the queen to b2 and now wants to put the rook in front.

   A) After 3...♕c2 4.e5 fxe5 5.fxe5 ♕f5 6.e6 ♗e8 7.♖f1 or 7.c4 it is hard to offer Black any good advice;

   B) Better was 3...a4 4.♗c4 ♖b7 5.♖ad1 ♕b6=.

4.e5! ♖fe8

Already it is obvious that White has a large advantage.

5.♖ab1 ♖b2?! 6.♗c4± fxe5 7.fxe5 ♖f8 8.e6±

8.♖f1!+−.

8...♗a4 9.♖f1! ♖xb1 10.♖xb1 ♗c2 11.♖b7 ♖e8 12.g4 ♕a4 13.♕f4 ♖f8 14.♖b8! 1-0

Conclusion: Quickly develop your play in the area of the board where you are stronger; at the same time, in the area where the opponent is stronger, use all possible means to try to prevent him realising his plan.

Human nature revolts against planless activity. – Sergey Makarichev

The game is equal. The position is very complicated. Although Black has an extra piece, because of the weakness of the back rank he needs to seek equality.

In Ibraev-S.Guliev (Petropavlovsk 1999) play continued:

1...♕e3+ 2.♔h1

2.♔f1 ♕f4+=.

2...♘d6!

Forced. After 2...♖f8? 3.♖xf8+ ♔xf8 4.♖d8+ ♔e7 5.♕e8 Black is mated.

3.exd6??

Instead the logical continuation was 3.♖8xd6! ♘g4! 4.♗d4! ♘f2+ (dangerous was 4...♕f4? 5.♗g1! ♖xe5 6.♖d8 ♕xe4 7.♖xe8+ ♖xe8 8.♖d4!, obtaining a material advantage) 5.♔g1 ♘h3+ 6.♔h1 (weak was 6.♔f1? ♕f4+ 7.♔e2 ♕xe4+ 8.♔d2 ♕xg2+−+) 6...♘f2+ and Black gives perpetual check.

3...♖xd8 4.h3 ♘g4 5.♗c1 ♖exd6 6.♗xe3 ♖xd1+ 7.♔g1 ♖xg1+ 8.♔xg1 ♖d1+ 0-1

Conclusion: Flight is just a battle against falling.

More often than not, the exit is where the entrance was. – S.Lec

Solution 137

Solution 138

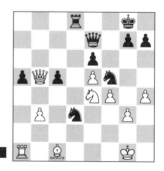

In the game Inarkiev-S.Guliev (Cimkent 1999), Black, having calculated the variation **1...♘xg3!! 2.♘xg3 ♕xh4 3.♔g2 ♘e1+ 4.♔f2 ♕h2+ 5.♔xe1 ♕xg3+ ♔e2**, saw that the black rook cannot join in the attack because of the mate on e8. However, Black missed he could win by **4...♘c2!** (threatening 5...♕h2+ with ...♘d4+ or ...♖d1# next) **5.♔g2 ♘xa1**. Therefore he chose the quiet:

1...h6

Creating a bolthole for the king. The game continued as follows:

2.♕xa5?!

After this, Black's attack becomes even sharper! He should have played 2.♗d2 ♕f7 (also principled is 2...♘xg3 3.♘xg3 ♕xh4 4.♔g2 ♘xf4+ 5.♗xf4 ♕xf4 6.♕c4 (6.♖e1!?) 6...♖d2+ (6...♕xe5 7.♖xa5 ♕e3=) 7.♔h3 ♕xe5 8.♖xa5 ♕e3, and we reach a position which is difficult to assess, but looks about equal. However, it is also worth considering the calm 2...♔h7!?) 3.♕xa5 (3.♗xa5 ♖d4 with a strong initiative for the pawn for Black) 3...♕d7 4.♕c3 ♕e8 (4...♕c6!? with unclear play) 5.♕a5 ♕d7 6.♕c3 ♕e8 – in Houdini's opinion, the players should repeat the position. Most likely, the position does not exceed the bounds of equality.

2...♕d7!∓ 3.♔h2 ♕d5 4.♗d2?

4...♔h7!

Another prophylactic move; the immediate 4...♕xe4 5.♕xd8+ ♔h7 6.♕a8! ♕e2+ 7.♕g2! is good for White.

5.♘c3 ♕f3 6.♖g1 ♘f2

By sacrificing the rook, Black goes over to a mating attack. 6...♘xe5! wins as well.

7.♕xd8 ♘xg3! 8.♗e1 ♘f1+ 9.♖xf1 ♕h3+ 10.♔g1 ♕g3#

Conclusion: The target is the king!

When attacking on opposite flanks, one must not forget about prophylaxis. –Yuri Razuvaev

Solution 139

It looks at first as though Black has managed to establish a fortress – the white king cannot break through. Even so, White is winning. He transfers the bishop to f8, placing Black in zugzwang, enters with his king and wins.

In the game S.Guliev-Gorin (Koszalin 1999) White executed this plan in the following manner:

69.♗h6 ♗c6 70.♔d3

Gaining time on the clock.

70...♔d5 71.♗f8 ♗e8 72.♔c3 ♔c5

'Shoulder-charging' his opposite number – he cannot let the white king get to a5.

73.b3!

This is the move which decides the fate of the game. Black cannot hold back the enemy king.

73...♔c6 74.♔b4 ♔b6 75.♗h6 ♗f7 76.♗e3+ ♔c6 77.♔a4 ♗e8 78.♔a5 ♔b7 79.b4 ♗d7 80.b5 ♗e8 81.♔b4 ♗d7 82.♔c5 ♗e8 83.b6

And here Black resigned – he cannot prevent the white king reaching the f8-square.

Conclusion: Sometimes a quiet pawn move at the end of the game can decide matters!

Everyone who wishes to master the endgame should understand that, in this phase of the game, playing skill often takes second place behind exact knowledge. At the board, in conditions of limited thinking time, it can sometimes be impossible to find the only winning path, if one does not know it. – Yuri Averbakh

Solution 140

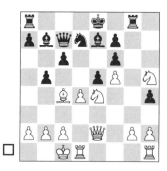

In the game L.Guliev-Mirzoev (Baku 1999) Black fell behind in development after some careless moves in the opening. His position is now seriously compromised. But an advantage in development is a dynamic advantage, and in order to get benefit from it, one must hurry!

17.dxe5! fxe5

Bad is 17...bxc4 because of 18.exf6, whilst after 17...♕xe5 or 17...♘xe5 White wins with 18.♘exf6+.

18.♖xd7! ♔xd7 19.♗xf7 ♗g5+?

In a hopeless position, Black commits another mistake. 'In a bad position, mistakes come easily!'

20.♘xg5 ♖xg5 21.♕d2+ 1-0

Conclusion: A good opening is half the job.

A bad start leads to a bad end. –Publius Terentius

Solution 141

Black is ready to deprive White of his main trump – the two bishops. But the direct decision, e.g. 15...♗xc4 16.♕xc4 ♖c8 17.♕a6! or 15...♖c8 16.♗xd5 ♕xd5 17.♕a4 (17.♕xd5 ♘xd5 18.♖fc1±) 17...♕b7 18.b5!, would leave White with strong pressure.

In the game S.Guliev-Gashimov (Baku 1999) Black demonstrated his mastery of prophylactic play, with

15...b5!

equalising immediately. After

16.♗xd5 ♕xd5 17.♕xd5 ♘xd5 18.♖fc1 ♖fc8

the position becomes drawish. Did you solve this example easily? If so, this means that you are well-acquainted with the technique of playing on squares of one colour and also the theories of Philidor and Capablanca regarding the placing of pawns.

Conclusion: It is essential to be able to handle the pawns.

... all the battles on the chessboard can usefully be seen through the prism of strategy, which in itself largely comes down to the evolution of the pawn structure. – Igor Zaitsev

Solution 142

It seems that White has some advantage. With his last move (♖a1-a4) he prepared to double rooks on the a-file and also took control of the fourth rank, preventing Black organising a pawn storm on the kingside. However, connoisseurs of the Benoni structure will not be fooled! Black stands better.
In the game S.Guliev-Guseinov (Baku 1999) the following black move came as a cold shower to his opponent!
19...a5!

After long thought, White decided to go for the main line.
20.bxa6?
Now Black gets a promising position. Standing still is dangerous, as in this position, Black's kingside play develops without hindrance. The immediate 20.f4 gxf4 favours Black after 21.♖axf4 ♗h6, but by means of 20.♕c2, White could prevent the advance ...f5-f4. It is also worth considering 21.gxf4 (instead of 21.♖axf4) 21...♘g6 22.e4 with a very complicated position.
20...b5!
The key move of the combination.
21.♖aa1
After 21.♘xb5 ♖fb8 or 21...♖ab8 Black obtains a material advantage.
21...b4 22.♘d1 ♖xa6 23.♖xa6 ♘xa6 24.♘e3 f4! 25.gxf4 gxf4 26.♘c4 ♘c7
And Black's advantage assumed clear proportions.

Conclusion: En passant captures are not always dangerous.

Sow an action, reap a habit, sow a habit, reap a character, sow a character, reap the fate. – William Thackeray

Solution 143

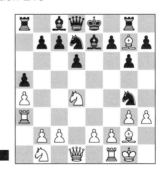

The position is very sharp and non-standard. Black faces a difficult choice.

In the game S.Guliev-Koketchov (Kiev 1999) he preferred to take the pawn and after the moves
11...♘xf2? 12.♖xf2 ♖xg7 13.♖xf7!! ♖xf7
(nor is he saved after 13...♔xf7 14.♗d5+ ♔f6 15.♖f3+ ♔e5 16.♘e6)
14.♘e6 c6 15.♘xd8 ♔xd8 16.♖f3
White obtained an overwhelming advantage, which he subsequently realised.

The continuation 11...♘ge5 12.♗h6 also gives White a serious advantage.

The strongest continuation was
11...♖xg7! 12.hxg4 ♘e5 13.g5 c6,
which leads to an unclear game. This game probably reminded you of the famous game Fischer-Reshevsky (New York 1958).

Conclusion: There is no future without a past.

The chief method of improvement in chess is studying the games of masters. – Siegbert Tarrasch

Solution 144

With his last move 17...a6, Black set a trap. White should have replied

18.♖e5 and accepted that the position is completely equal.
But anyone who thought White can play
18.♖xb7??
as played in the game S.Guliev-Vaulin (Tula 1999), was badly mistaken, since after the reply
18...0-0-0!
White can only resign. Grandmasters are also just humans and sometimes miss the simplest things! They also need from time to time to look at simple combinations.

Conclusion: In what circumstances can a king move 2 squares, rather than just 1?

Castling can also be a threat!

Solution 145

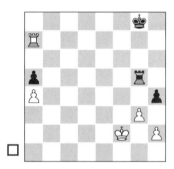

In the game S.Guliev-Tolstykh (Nizhny Novgorod 1999) there followed:
49.gxh4 ♖c5 50.h3 ♔f8 51.♔g3 ♖c3+ 52.♔g4 ♖c4+ 53.♔g5 ♖xa4 54.h5 ♖a1??
54...♖a3 55.h4 (55.♔g6 ♖g3+ 56.♔h7 ♖xh3 57.♖xa5 ♔f7 58.h6 ♖f3=) 55...♔g8 56.♔g6 (56.h6 ♔h8) 56...♖g3+=.
55.♔g6

White could win with 55.h6! ♔g8 56.h7+ ♔h8 57.♔h6.

55...♖g1+ 56.♔h7 ♖a1

And the players soon agreed a draw. Also possible was 56...♖g3 and 56...♖g5!?.

Another interesting try was 49.♔f3 hxg3 50.hxg3 ♖f5+ 51.♔e4! ♖g5 (51...♖c5 52.♖d7 and then ♖d4) 52.♔f4 ♖c5 53.♖e7 and ♖e4, because the rook defends both pawns along the rank, White could obtain what looks like a theoretically winning position. However, today's tablebases teach us differently!

The 'winning' plan is described by Panchenko in his book *Theory and Practice of Chess Endings*:

If the weaker side's king is in front of the passed pawn, then the stronger side begins an attack on the enemy pawns on the other flank, using his passed pawn as a deflection.

By way of an example, he presents a position from the game Damjanovic-Hutteman (Dortmund 1974).

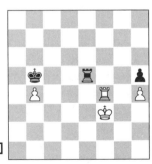

White's plan consists in the exchange of the b4-pawn for that on h5. The game continued as follows:

47.♖d4 ♔c6

Or 47...♔a4 48.♔f4 ♖b5 49.♖d1! ♔b3 (49...♖xb4+ 50.♔g5 ♖b5+ 51.♔g6 and then ♖d1-g1-g5+–) 50.♖g1 ♔c3 51.♖g5 ♖xb4+ 52.♔g3 ♖b1 53.♖xh5 and White wins according to Panchenko. However, the tablebase is inexorable: 53...♔d4 achieves a draw!

48.♔f4 ♖b5 49.♔e4 ♔b6 50.♖c4 ♔b7 51.♔f4 ♔b6 52.♔f3! ♖f5+ 53.♔e4 ♖b5 54.♔f4

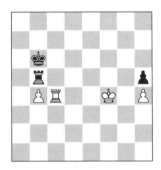

54...♖d5

54...♔b7 55.♖c5! ♖xb4+ 56.♔g5 seems winning for White, but after 56...♔b6 57.♖e5 ♔c6 58.♔xh5 ♔d6, Black reaches a theoretically drawn position.

55.♖c8! ♖d4+ 56.♔g5 ♔b7 57.♖c5 ♖xb4 58.♔xh5 ♔b6 59.♖c3 ♖b1 60.♔h6 ♖h1 61.h5 ♖h2 62.♔g6 ♖g2+ 63.♔f6 ♖h2 64.♔g5 ♖h1 65.h6 1-0

By analogy with this example, in our case White needs to exchange his g-pawn for the black pawn on a5. And then, having cut off the black king as far away as possible, he advances the a-pawn. Unfortunately for White, he missed this chance, although also in this case, after a tough defence, Black could still have held the draw.

Conclusion: Do not forget constantly to revise standard endgame positions!

... study first of all the endgame, so as to appreciate better the capabilities of the pieces and develop a feeling for their cooperation. – José Raul Capablanca.

Solution 146

The first thing which strikes one's eyes is White's two bishops, pointing at the black king. However, lovers of defence, who have Olympian calm, may notice some hidden defensive possibilities for Black. If we add to these his strong initiative on the queenside, which is greatly helped by the ♘d4, then, taking into account all these factors, we can conclude that the position is equal.

In the game Jakubowski-S.Guliev (Koszalin 1999) there followed:

16...bxc4

16...♕e8 17.hxg6 hxg6 18.♕g4 bxc4 19.♗xg6 ♘f3+ 20.♔g2 ♘e5 21.♗xe8 ♘xg4 22.♗h5 ♘e5=.

17.hxg6 ♖f6

17...hxg6 18.♗xg6 is rather dangerous.

18.♕h5

White has evidently not guessed his opponent's idea, otherwise he would have chosen 18.gxh7+ ♔h8 19.♗d5 or 18.♗e3, although in both cases, Black has clear counterplay. **18...hxg6 19.♗xg6 ♖xg6! 20.♕xg6 ♕f8 21.♕g4?!**

21.♗e3!±.

21...♕f3 22.♕xf3 ♘xf3+ 23.♔g2 ♘d4

And Black has the easier play.

Conclusion: The most difficult thing is to understand the opponent's ideas. This is vital in the heat of battle!

A real player is good not only at attacking but also at solidly meeting the enemy's play. – Yury Kotkov

Solution 147

At first glance, White has a strong initiative. If 15...g4 16.♘h4 ♕xd4 17.♕xd4 ♗xd4 18.♖xe7 his position deserves preference. However, Black has good counterplay with the help of some tactical nuances. The assessment is that the position is equal.

In the game Chekhov-S.Guliev (Moscow 1999) Black, with

15...♗g4 16.♕e4?! ♕f5!

even seized the initiative, since White cannot play 17.♕xe7 ♖f7 18.♕xd6 ♗f8, trapping the queen.

After
17.♘d2
the players agreed a draw.

Conclusion: Even monarchs need calmness!

Thought and fantasy inevitably come first. Behind them is scientific calculation, and, in the end, execution crowns the idea. – Konstantin Tsiolkovsky

Solution 148

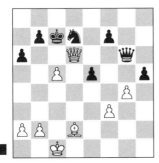

Black is not better and he needs to defend in order to save the game. At first glance, the exchange of queens is very dangerous for Black, because it allows White to obtain an outside passed pawn. In a battle between a bishop and a knight in the endgame, this usually gives the bishop a large advantage.
In the game Goloschapov-S.Guliev (Nyzhny Novgorod 1999) Black followed this rule and believed his opponent, playing
33...♚d8?
but after
34.♗a5+ ♚e8 35.♕c7 ♕g5+ 36.♚d1
he quickly lost. But it was precisely in the endgame that he had good drawing chances! The game is

equal. By means of **33...♕xd6 34.cxd6+ ♚xd6 35.gxh5 ♘f6 36.h6 ♘h7 37.♚c2 f5 38.♚d3 ♚d5** Black could have easily maintained the balance, thanks to his active centralised king.

Conclusion: A centralised king in the endgame is a clear advantage!

In the middle of the game, the king is only a spectator, but in the endgame, he is one of the main actors. – Aron Nimzowitsch

Solution 149

The white pawn on d5 and the black one on e4 are cut off from their bases. Black is ready to strengthen his pawn with the move ...f7-f5 and then to mobilise his forces on the queenside, organising a kingside attack. White is not able to give such support to his d5-pawn. At first glance, Black has the advantage. However, White has the possibility of opening the game, whilst he is ahead in development. Therefore it is White who has the better game.
In the game S.Guliev-Djachkov (Nyzhny Novgorod 1999) there followed the energetic
18.f4! exf3

After 18...♕f6 19.♘e3 followed by ♕d2, ♖ac1, ♖f1 and g3-g4, White gets superiority all over the board. **19.exf3 ♕f6 20.g4!?**
Even stronger was 20.♕d2! with the idea of playing b3-b4, a2-a3 etc. **20...♔g8 21.♕d2 ♗d7 22.♘g3**
And now better was 22.b4!, but even without this, it is clear that White's position deserves preference.

Conclusion: One must always be ready for the opening of the game!

Time and tide wait for no man.

Solution 150

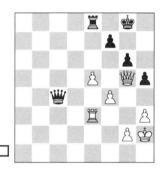

It seems as though Black has managed to create an unbreachable fortress. However, White has an interesting resource at his disposal. By returning the extra pawn, he can take play by force into a winning pawn endgame! White has a decisive advantage.
In the game S.Guliev-Chekhov (Koszalin 1999) play continued **35.f5! ♕c2 36.e6! ♕xf5 37.♕xf5 gxf5 38.exf7+ ♔xf7 39.♖xe8 ♔xe8 40.♔g3 ♔f7 41.♔f4 ♔f6 42.h4!** (but not 42.g3?? h4! with a draw) **42...♔e6 43.♔g5 ♔e5 44.♔xh5** and Black resigned.

Conclusion: Calculation of variations is extremely important, even in the endgame.

Pawn endings are the basis of the entire endgame. – Alexander Panchenko

Solution 151

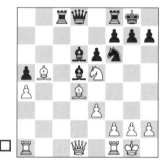

After
1.♕e2
in the game S.Guliev-Vaulin (Karaganda 1999) Black won a pawn with:
1...♗xg2! 2.♔xg2 ♗xe5 3.♗xe5 ♕d5+
The position is equal. Black's central pressure should have been fought against by means of **1.f3** (but not 1.♖c1? ♖xc1 2.♕xc1 ♗xg2!; nor is 1.♘g4 ♘e4 impressive) **1...♕c7 2.♖c1 ♕b8** (after 2...♕xc1 3.♕xc1 ♖xc1 4.♖xc1, thanks to the weakness of the a5-pawn and control of the c-file, White has a positional advantage) **3.♖xc8 ♖xc8 4.♕a1! ♗c5!**. Thus Black removes the strong ♗d4.

Conclusion: Watch out – double attack!

Only a blow directed backwards gives a person full frontal force. – Stefan Zweig

Solution 152

The position of the black king is very weak, and it seems as though the white queen is not inferior to the two rooks in this position, and maybe even outguns them. A simple but nice tactical blow comes to Black's aid. His position is winning. The game Hamzin-S.Guliev (Petropavlovsk 1999) continued **1...♖xb2+! 2.♔xb2** (nothing changes after 2.♕xb2 ♖b5) **2...♖b5+ 3.♕xb5 cxb5 4.♔c3 ♔c7** and Black soon won.

Conclusion: Always look for the chance of a tactical blow!

Solution 153

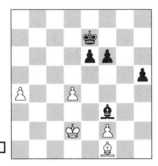

A difficult situation. Both sides have an outside passed pawn. It seems as though the cooperation of king and bishop (plus the fact that it is his move) gives White the advantage, but

this is not the case. The position is equal. Let us look at the variations:

A) 1.a5 ♗c6! (1...♔d6 is also possible, but the variations 1...e5? 2.♗e2! ♗xe2 3.♔xe2 ♔d6 4.a6 ♔c6 5.d5!+− and 1...h4? 2.♔e3 ♗c6 3.♔f4 followed by ♔g4+− favour White) 2.♔c3 ♔d6 3.♔c4 h4= − it is not clear how White can strengthen his position;

B) After 1.♗e2 ♗c6! (1...♗xe2? 2.♔xe2 ♔d6 3.♔f3! ♔d5 4.♔g3! leads to a win for White) 2.a5 h4 each side's passed pawn cancels the other out – the position is a draw. In the game S.Guliev-Vaulin (Karaganda 1999) play continued:
1.♔e3 ♗c6!
As we will see, in many variations, this tempo gain comes to Black's aid just in time.
2.a5 e5!
After 2...♔d6 3.♗e2 h4 4.♔f4 Black would have some worries, although here too, after 4...♗d7 nothing is threatened. With the text move Black does not cede space.
3.f4
This eases Black's game, but even after the strongest move 3.dxe5 fxe5 4.♗d3 h4 5.♗e4 ♔d6! (5...♗xe4? 6.♔xe4 ♔d6 7.♔f3 ♔c6 8.♔g4 ♔b5 9.♔xh4 ♔xa5 10.♔g5+−) 6.a6 ♗xe4 7.♔xe4 ♔c6 8.♔f3 ♔b6 9.♔g4 ♔xa6 10.♔xh4 ♔b5 11.♔g5 ♔c5 12.♔f5 ♔d5 the position is equal.
3...exd4+ 4.♔xd4 ♔d6 5.♔e3 ♔c5 6.♔f2 h4 7.♔g1 ♗d7 8.♔h2 ♗c8 9.♔g2 ♗g4 10.♔f2 ♗f5 11.♔f3 ♗c8 ♔f2
And the players agreed a draw.

Conclusion: Can we sometimes anticipate our own mistakes?

The reward for doing one's duty is the chance to do the next duty. – George Eliot

Solution 154

Here in the game Grigoriants-S. Guliev (Moscow 2000) there followed
1.♖d3?
and after
1...f5 2.b3 axb3 3.♖xb3 g4 4.♖b6+
(4.f4 d4!)
4...♚e5 5.fxg4 fxg4 6.♚b2 ♚e4 7.♚b3 g3 8.a4 g2
White did not find after 9.♖g6 ♚f3 any defence to 10...♖g4 and so resigned.
The following day, Grigoriants showed an original way to draw for White, which both players had missed during the game. The diagram position is drawn: **1.♖xc4!** **dxc4 2.♚c2 f5 3.♚d2 g4 4.♚e2!**
and White has managed to build a fortress, which Black cannot breach. If he takes too many liberties, he can even lose, e.g. 4...♚d5 5.♚f2! c3? 6.bxc3 ♚c4 7.e4!+−.
At the board Black did not see 4.♚e2!, being convinced that, thanks to his outside passed pawn, the endgame was a win. However, as we see, we have an exception to the usual rule! If there were a

player in the world who knew every exception to the chess rules, he would probably be unbeatable.

Conclusion: Exceptions and rules are relatives, and we can only guess at the precise link.

Pawn endings are relatively rare in practice. People avoid them. They are not known and not loved. It is no secret that pawn endings are terra incognita even to many masters, grandmasters and World Champions. – Nikolai Grigoriev

Solution 155

It is not difficult to see that the white knights are aiming at control of the e5-square. If they land there, Black will suffer. But he has available an original counterblow, thanks to which he obtains the advantage.
In the game Plasman-S.Guliev (Hoogeveen 2001), by means of the unexpected
16...e5!
Black managed to open the game in his favour.
17.fxe5
Or 17.♘gxe5!? f6 18.d4 cxd4 19.cxd4 fxe5 20.dxe5 (20.fxe5 ♗h6) 20...♘cb4! with advantage to Black.
17...h5! 18.♘f2 ♘xe5 19.♘xe5 ♖xe5 20.♕c4 ♖xe1+ 21.♖xe1 ♘f6

And Black's advantage became serious.

Conclusion: The centre must be either seized or controlled.

The initiative is closely connected with the gain of time, and the position in the centre determines the plan for the preparation and development of the attack in the middlegame, etc. – Alexander Koblencs

Solution 156

White is winning. In the game S.Guliev-Novrouzi (Teheran 2001) White used a standard tactical trick, which ensures him at least an extra exchange.
11.♘b5!
A characteristic knight jump for the Carlsbad structure. Black has fallen for this in many games over the years, including, for example, Olafsson-Poulsen (Helsinki Olympiad 1952). This tactical trick needs to be remembered!

Conclusion: The cramped position of the major pieces, especially the queen, is a good motif for a combination.

Traps should be outlawed by the police. – Savielly Tartakower

Solution 157

During the game L.Guliev-Dovliatov (Baku 2001) both sides were happy with their position. Black is ready to occupy the h-file and create an attack on the enemy king. On the other hand, the insecure position of Black's king and the unfortunate position of his queen give White good prospects of counterplay. White is better.
38.♘f5+!
It is in precisely such play that the knight can be very strong. The love of the white knight for the d5- and f5-squares in such structures should not be ignored!
38...gxf5 39.♖f3 ♕h6 40.♖h3 ♕f4 41.♖f3 ♕h6 42.♖h3 ♕f4 43.♖g3+!
White avoids the repetition, which is a very risky decision. In such positions, avoiding the draw requires considerable nerve. As the saying goes, 'Courage does not ask how high the rock is'.
43...♔f7 44.♕h5+ ♔e7 45.♖g7+ ♔d8 46.♖d1!
The threat is 47.g3, trapping the queen. In turn, the black king and queen become objects of attack for the white forces.
46...fxe4
Black could beat off the attack with a counter-sacrifice of the knight:

46...♘xe4! 47.♗xe4 ♗c8! (bad is 47...♕xe4? 48.♖xb7 ♕g4 49.♕h7! ♕xd1+ 50.♔h2) 48.♗c2 e4!. We have reached a very complicated and sharp position, where White's chances look preferable, but nothing real is apparent. However, 48.♗f3 is decisive. After 48...e4 49.♕h7 exf3 50.♖e1!, Black cannot prevent White entering the seventh rank by ♖ee7 and mate will soon follow.

47.♖g4!

Now White obtains a large advantage.

47...♔c7 48.♖xf4 exf4 49.axb5 axb5 50.♗xe4! ♖ae8 51.♕h7+ ♔b6 52.♗f3

White's advantage looks decisive. Black soon resigned.

Conclusion: Try to look at the position through the eyes of the opponent!

The enemy's eyes only look at you when you can see what is good and what is bad! – Nizami Gianjavi

Solution 158

If you are an aggressive player, who likes to take and develop the initiative, then you will certainly have found the answer. White's position is close to winning.

In the game S.Guliev-Rzai (Teheran 2001) White decided that his advantage was sufficiently great and with the move

1.f4!

went over to active operations. There followed:

1...a6 2.e5! b5

Or 2...dxe5 3.d6 ♘e6 4.fxe5!.

3.axb5!?

During the post-mortem, Rzai said that he thought 3.♘e4! was even stronger. The variations 3...bxc4 4.♘xf6+ ♗xf6 5.♗xf6 ♕d7 6.f5! dxe5 7.d6 ♖b6 8.fxg6 fxg6 9.dxc7 and 3...♘xe4 4.♗xd8 ♖bxd8 5.axb5 axb5 6.♗d3 prove that he was correct.

3...dxe5 4.d6! ♘xb5 5.♘xb5 axb5 6.♗xf6 ♗xf6

7.♗xf7+! ♔xf7 8.♕d5+ ♔g7 9.fxe5 ♖f8 10.exf6+ ♔h8 11.♖a7! ♖b6 12.♕d2!

And Black resigned.

Incidentally, White almost always has to play aggressively in such positions. After the slow 1.f3?! Black has available an interesting pawn sacrifice: 1...g5! 2.♗g3 ♘d7! 3.♗xd6 ♘e5, for which he obtains strong play on the dark squares by way of compensation.

Conclusion: In defence, the main thing is calmness – in attack, decisiveness!

Nothing great was ever achieved without enthusiasm. – Ralph Waldo Emerson

Solution 159

The game is equal. At first glance, White looks to be better because of his hegemony over the long black diagonal. However, with the help of a sharp counterattack, Black achieves equality.

In the game S.Guliev-Alizade (Babul 2001) there followed

1...♘h5!

and after the forced

2.g3

(2.♕c1 ♕g4) Black played a standard combination:

2...♘xf4! 3.gxf4 ♕g4+ 4.♔h1 ♕f3+

(4...♕xf4 5.♕d1 ♖xe4 6.♖f1! with unclear play)

5.♔g1 ♕g4+

and the players agreed a draw. In this example, we see the black forces working together effectively.

Conclusion: Never lose your objectivity!

In essence, the battle for the initiative is the basic law of chess. – Vlastimil Hort, Vlastimil Jansa

Solution 160

If you easily came to the conclusion that White stands better here, then you are clearly well-acquainted with positions of this type. The black central pawns do not have sufficient piece support. This factor plays the main role in the assessment of the position.

In the game L.Guliev-Bagirov (Abu Dhabi 2001) White obtained the advantage, by carrying out a characteristic break in such structures:

15.f5!

The great activity of the white pieces and Black's lack of development justify aggressive play. There was also a quieter alternative: 15.♗b5 ♘e7 16.♖he1 a6 17.♗f1 ♗d7 18.♘d4, which also promises White clearly the better game.

15...e5

Tempting is 15...♘e4, but here too, by means of 16.♘xe4 dxe4 17.♘h4 followed by ♗h3 White retains a large advantage.

16.♘xd5 ♗xf5 17.♗b5 ♗e4

Black tries to hold his difficult position with only moves, but he cannot succeed.

18.♗xc6 ♗xf3 19.♘e7+ ♔f7

20.♗xf3 e4 21.♘d5

163

It was worth considering 21.♗g2! ♔xe7 22.b4!.

21...exf3 22.♖hf1 ♖ad8 23.♖xf3

With a serious advantage to White.

Conclusion: In such pawn structures, one should always look for breaks.

In recent years, a number of older openings have undergone a reassessment. Enriched with new ideas, they are now increasingly seen in the games of top grandmasters. – Vasily Ivanchuk

Solution 161

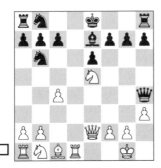

We have before us an example of a pawn sacrifice to gain a lead in development. It is not hard to see that White has sufficient compensation for the sacrificed material. Closer examination of the position reveals that White has the advantage! So as to come to this conclusion, it is important to see White's next move and assess its consequences.

12.c5!

Sacrificing yet another pawn, but already for an attack.

12...♗xc5

White would answer other moves in the same way.

13.♕b5+ ♘8d7 14.♘xd7 ♕xf2+ 15.♔h1 0-0-0 16.♘xb6+

16.♖f1!.

16...♗xb6 17.♖f1 ♕c2 18.♘c3

Although Black has three pawns for the piece, the superior activity of White's pieces makes his position more attractive. In the game L.Guliev-Olenderek (Koszalin 2001), after a long and mutually error-filled battle, White won.

Conclusion: The level of knowledge of one's stuff is the sign of mastery.

When two people do the same thing, it is not the same thing. (Latin proverb)

Solution 162

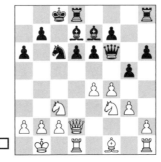

On the board is a characteristic Sicilian position. An experienced practitioner of this opening will soon note that White has the advantage. The main factor which determines this assessment is the poor position of the black queen. Usually in the Sicilian, its rightful place is c7. Black has castled queenside and the absence of his strongest piece from that wing makes it hard for him to defend the weak squares in the vicinity of the king.

Exploiting this circumstance, White, in the game L.Guliev-Gashimov (Baku 2001), quickly decided the game in his favour:
14.♕e3! ♕g7?!
Black defends against e4-e5, but the main threat was something else!
15.♕b6 ♘b8
He cannot allow 16.♗xa6.
16.♘d4 ♗e8 17.♗c4
And now the threat is 18.♗xe6.
17...♘d7 18.♕a5 ♘c5 19.b4!
White completely dominates the queenside.
19...♘xe4 20.♘xe4 d5 21.♘c5 dxc4 22.♘cxe6 1-0

Conclusion: One must not allow even one piece to lose its way!

There are openings in which successful defence by Black depends largely on whether he can satisfactorily develop one or other minor piece. Lovers of the French Defence, for example, know how much trouble they can have with their light-squared bishop, whilst King's Indian players often fret over a knight on a5. Spanish players frequently have great trouble with the knight cut off on the queenside. – Efim Geller

Solution 163

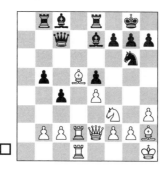

Before us is an example with which to train your tactical vision. The move 1.♗xf7+ is possible. But before deciding on such a move, one needs to calculate variations accurately and have a good feel for the attack!
1.♗xf7+ ♔xf7 2.♘xe5+ ♘xe5
3.♕h5+ g6
3...♔f8 4.♗xe5.
4.♕xh7+ ♔f8!
4...♔f6 5.♖d5!.
5.f4!
5.♗f4 g5 6.♗xg5 ♘f7 7.♗h6+ ♘xh6 8.♕xh6+ leads only to a draw.
5...♘f7
Also after 5...♗d6 6.♕h8+ ♔f7 7.♕h6 White has a very strong attack.
6.f5
Although Black has two extra pieces, White's attack more than compensates for the material deficit. In conditions of a practical game, such an attack is almost impossible to defend, if you are a human and not a computer.
A conscientious analysis of this position will undoubtedly bring you benefits. So as to get a better feeling for positions where one side has sacrificed material for an attack on the king, one needs to analyse many such examples.
In the game L.Guliev-Slapikas (Swidnice 2001) White unfortunately missed this interesting combination.

Conclusion: The road is open to the brave.

Just as we determine our behaviour, so our behaviour defines us. – George Eliot

Solution 164

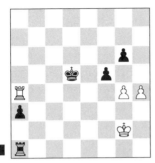

Black is winning: **54...fxg4! 55.♔g3** (55.♖xg4 ♖b1) **55...♔c5! 56.♔g2 ♔b5**, and later the king hides from the checks on a2 and Black wins easily.

However, in the game Dizdar-S. Guliev (Abu Dhabi 2001) Black was fixated on the idea of creating a passed pawn on the f-file, completely forgetting that the a-pawn was already on the third rank and the black king had a flight square on a2. In such a situation, and with a pawn on the g-file, Black wins. The game went:

54...♔e6? 55.h5!

Black had completely forgotten about this possibility.

55...gxh5 56.♖a6+!

An important intermediate check. 56.gxh5 ♔f6! or 56.gxf5+ ♔xf5 lead to a winning position for Black, but now, if the black king flees to the fifth rank, then it is cut off and cannot help stop the h-pawn; he would have to give up the a-pawn for it. And if the king retreats to the seventh rank, there follows the simple gxf5 and we have a theoretically drawn position.

56...♔e5 57.gxh5 ♔f4 58.h6 ♖a2+ 59.♔h3 ♖a1

And a draw was agreed.

Conclusion: Obsession is a dangerous enemy!

One should never become a slave to one's desires. – Aron Nimzowitsch

Solution 165

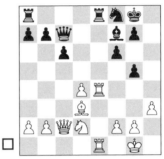

The white pieces are actively placed and the light squares in the black king's residency are weakened. On the other hand, White has an IQP on d4. After the exchange of a few pieces (Black is already threatening to exchange rooks) this can cause White a serious headache.

All this shows that White needs to get on with active means.

In the game S.Guliev-Lodkhi (Abu Dhabi 2001) White played

24.d5!

which ensured him the advantage. After

24...♖xe4

(24...c5 25.b4 b6 26.♖xe8 ♖xe8 27.♖xe8 ♗xe8 28.♘e4!)

25.♗xe4 ♖e8 26.♖c1! ♕a5 27.dxc6 bxc6 28.b3

White's advantage becomes obvious.

Conclusion: An unblockaded isolani can advance at any moment.

He who fears an isolated pawn should not play chess. – Siegbert Tarrasch

Solution 166

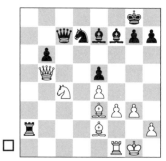

White's positional superiority is not in doubt. This is evidently why Black, with his last move (24...♖a8-a2), decided to provoke tactical complications. By means of 25.♗d3 White could avoid any trouble and retain his advantage, but the main question nonetheless is: can he take on b6?

25.♘xb6!? ♖xe2!? 26.♖c1 ♕xc1+!?
After other replies, White, by taking on e2, keeps a large advantage, e.g. 26...♕b7 27.♕xe2 (or 27.♖c8+ ♗f8 28.♕xd7 ♕a6 29.♖xf8+ ♔xf8 30.♗c5+, mating) 27...♘xb6 28.♕b5 ♗d8 29.♖b1. It seems unlikely, but during the game, Black overlooked the possibility of 26...♕xc1+!.

27.♗xc1 ♗c5+ 28.♔f1
28.♔h1? ♖e1+ 29.♔g2 ♖g1+ 30.♔h3 ♗e6+ 31.g4 ♗xb6−+.

28...♖c2 29.♘xd7?
29.♕xd7! ♖xc1+ 30.♔e2 ♗xb6 31.♕b7! and White wins: thanks to the back-rank mate threat, Black loses one of his bishops.
In the game S.Guliev-Ulibin (Abu Dhabi 2001) both players in their preliminary calculations missed 31.♕b7. Ulibin pointed this out in the post-mortem.

29...♗c4+ 30.♕xc4+ ♖xc4 31.♗b2 ♗a7 32.♗xe5 ♖c2

But now it was Black who obtained the advantage, although after a long battle, White succeeded in making a draw.

Conclusion: Every action has a start and a finish. So that the finish can be successful, one must work hard from the very start!

All long variations are wrong. – Bent Larsen

Solution 167

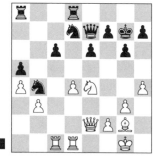

White's advantage is not in doubt. In the event of quiet play, White will transfer the knight to c4 and gradually strengthen his pressure on the black position all over the board.
Foreseeing this, in the game S.Guliev-Bagirov (Biel 2001), Black, with the move

24...e5

decided to exploit the less-than-ideal position of the white queen and knight on the same file. This is refuted by an original tactical manoeuvre. There followed:

25.♘d2! ♕f6 26.♗xc6!
Black probably overlooked this blow.

26...♘xc6 27.♘e4 ♘xd4
27...♕e6 28.d5.

28.♖xd4 ♕e7 29.♖d5
White has managed to further increase his positional advantage.
29...♘f8
Probably the most tenacious here was 29...♘f6, settling for the loss of a pawn, although it is only right to add that, in this case, White would have had every chance of winning.
30.♕b5 ♖db8
30...♖xd5 31.♕xd5 and ♖c5.
31.♖xe5 ♕a3
31...♖xb5 32.♖xe7 ♖xb3 33.♖cc7.
32.♕c5 ♕xb3 33.♖e7 ♘e6 34.♕e5+ ♔g8 35.♘f6+ ♔f8 36.♘xh7+ ♔g8 37.♘f6+ ♔f8 38.♘d5 ♕b2 39.♖c8+
And Black resigned.

Conclusion: The opposition of major pieces is often the harbinger of a decisive battle.

Where there are no good moves, an oversight often results. – Siegbert Tarrasch

Solution 168

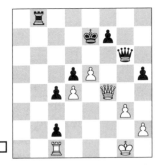

White's position looks completely cheerless, but he has a tactical possibility which allows him to draw by force. The game is equal. The game S.Guliev-Miton (Ohrid 2001) continued:
33.♖xc2! ♕xc2

The assessment is not changed by 33...♖b1+ 34.♖c1 ♖xc1+ (34...♖b2 35.♖a1) 35.♕xc1 ♕d3 (35...♕e4 36.♕a3+) 36.♕f4=.
34.♕f6+ ♔f8 35.♕h8+ ♔e7 36.♕f6+ ♔e8 37.♕h8+ ♔e7 38.♕f6+
And the players agreed a draw. White's play reminds one of a drowning man clutching at a straw. Sometimes such miracle cures work!

Conclusion: In comfortable conditions, everyone can fight, but in inferior circumstances, only a few.

... only one thing needs to be taken into account: the course of events. – Antoine de Saint-Exupéry

Solution 169

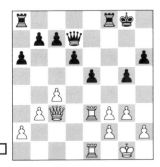

In 'direct' variations, it is not easy to exploit White's advantage. On the other hand, if he dawdles, Black will double his rooks on the f-file and organise a dangerous attack on the white king. In the game S.Guliev-Duman (Izmir 2002), White, by developing an initiative on both flanks, created weaknesses in the enemy pawn structure and obtained the advantage:

21.c5! ♕c6 22.h4!

After the immediate 22.cxd6 cxd6 or 22...♕xc3 23.♖xc3 cxd6 24.♖c7 ♖f7 25.♖ec1 ♖af8 White has nothing.

22...♖f5

The problem is not solved by 22...gxh4 23.♕c4+ ♔g7 24.♕g4+ ♔h7 25.♕xh4 ♕xc5 26.♕e7+ ♔h8 (26...♔g8 27.♖e4) 27.♖xe5+–.

23.hxg5 hxg5 24.♕d2! ♕xc5 25.♖c1 25.♖c3!?.

25...♕d4 26.♖d3 ♕b6 27.♖dc3 ♖f7 28.♖c4! ♖af8 29.♖g4 ♖g7 30.♕d5+ ♖ff7 31.♕e6 c5 32.♖d1 ♕c6 33.♖d5

And White's advantage became obvious. White tried to follow the well-known principle:

My favourite strategy is playing on both wings. – Alexander Alekhine

Conclusion: One must learn to look at the whole board at once.

Solution 170

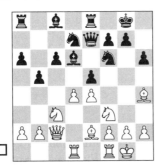

White's pieces are better developed. As a consequence, the initiative belongs to him. But how can he develop it? This question always comes to mind in positions with such a plan.

In the game S.Guliev-Gelashvili (Izmir 2002) White answered the question with the move:

15.♔h1!

The point of this retreat is to transfer the move to Black! It is a unique case – there are 15 black pieces on the board and the position is not closed by any means, and yet Black does not have a useful move! For example, if 15...♗b7, then 16.dxe5 ♘xe5 17.♘d4!; little better is 15...♖b8 16.dxe5 ♘xe5 17.♖xd6 or 15...exd4 16.♘xd4 ♘e5 17.f4 etc. In such cases, it is said that the threat is stronger than its execution. At the board, after

15...b4 16.♘a4 exd4 17.♕xc6 ♖a7 18.♖xd4 ♗e5 19.♘xe5 ♕xe5 20.♕c4 ♘xe4 21.♗f3 ♖c7 22.♕d3 ♘dc5 23.♘xc5 ♘xc5 24.♕d2 ♖d7 25.♖xd7 ♗xd7 26.♗g3 ♕f5 27.♕xb4

White achieved an obvious advantage.

The most subtle moves are waiting moves! – Aron Nimzowitsch

Solution 171

White has a large advantage. The reason consists in the fact that Black does not have a 'normal' post for the bishop on f5. Exploiting this nuance, in the game S.Guliev-Erdogan (Izmit 2002) White went over to a decisive assault:

15.e4! ♗g6?!

After this, the bishop is in danger of being trapped! Of course, after either 15...dxe3 16.♗xe3 or 15...♗e6 16.♘xe6 fxe6 it is not a bed of roses for Black, but even so, he should have chosen one of these continuations.

16.♗d2

This move completes the development of the pieces and prevents the move 16...♘a5. Now the queen on b3 feels that she is boss of the position.

16...b6?!

Black does not feel the danger.

17.♖ac1 ♖ad8? 18.h4! d3 19.h5 ♘d4 20.♕xd3 ♗xh5 21.♘xh5 ♕g4 22.♘f4

And White soon won.

Conclusion: Attention – the opponent has a bad piece!

When shooting, one must aim above the target. – Franz Kafka

Solution 172

On the queenside, the black pawns have advanced threateningly far, and on this side of the board, there can be no doubt about his superiority. However, in the centre and on the kingside White can organise a strong attack. Because

of his lack of a dark-squared bishop, Black will not find this easy to repulse. White has a large advantage.

18.e5! ♘e8 19.♖e4!

White sacrifices a piece, in return for which he gets a powerful initiative on the kingside.

19...c3 20.♘xc3 bxc3 21.♗xc3 ♘b7

21...♖b5 22.♖a4.

22.♕h6 f6 23.e6 ♗d3 24.♖d4

It was worth considering 24.♖h4 g5 25.♖g4!?.

24...♗f5 25.g4 ♘g7

25...♗c2 26.♖c1; 25...♕c7 26.♖c1.

26.♕d2 ♘xe6 27.dxe6 ♗xe6 28.♖e1

With an obvious advantage.
This happened in the game S.Guliev-Reyhan (Izmit 2002). A day later, the young Turkish player told me that he had checked the game with the computer. Up to the move 19.♖e4! everything had been seen before and the rook move was a novelty, which changes the assessment of the entire variation. He also said that the computer did not consider this move and assesses the whole line as better for Black. But as soon as one puts this move on the screen, the computer, after a short think, starts assessing the position as almost winning for White.

This is an example where we can clearly see the difference between creative, human thinking, based on experience and understanding of the fundamental laws of chess, and the routine approach of the computer. Probably in the near future, in the search for ways to fight against the computer, positions of this type will be the subject of further research.

Conclusion: Every time has its own decree.

To understand is to feel. – Konstantin Stanislavsky

Solution 173

Probably you were rather shocked by the simplicity of this test? The game has only just begun and the position is equal.
8...♘h5??
occurred in the game Ipek-S.Guliev (Izmit 2002). After
9.♗xb8! ♖xb8 10.♘e5 ♘f6 11.♘c6
Black is an exchange down, with no compensation. Black, after making his move, had barely taken his hand off the piece, when he realised his mistake. But he had already made the move, and rules are rules!

Conclusion: You should not make active moves without having developed all your pieces!

Thinking is the hardest work of all, which is probably why so few people do it. – Henry Ford

Solution 174

The position requires a non-standard decision. White has exchanged his light-squared bishop for a knight and now plans to carry out the 'reverse' exchange – his knight for the opponent's light-squared bishop. But he has not yet completed his development, and in the game Mamedyarov-S.Guliev (Izmit 2002) Black showed that he has every right to fight for the initiative. There followed
10...c5
and after
11.♘xf5 gxf5 12.♕h5 cxd4 13.0-0-0!
(Black had completely forgotten about this possibility!)
13...e6
(13...♕a5!)
14.g4! f4 15.♘xe4 ♘c6 16.exd4 ♕a5 17.d5
the white attack had become irresistible and Black resigned. However, the position is equal! Black should have played **10...e6!**

11.♘xf5 exf5 12.♕c2 (12.0-0?! c5!) **12...c5 13.d5 ♕d6! 14.0-0 ♘d7** and then ...♘e5=. And after 11.g3 c5! Black even seizes the initiative.

Conclusion: Do not forget that castling is possible on both sides!

The biggest defeat is to lose control of yourself. – Democritus

Solution 175

The position is sharp and dynamic and therefore requires a concrete approach.
The move played in the game was a mistake and Black exploited this to obtain an advantage with the help of an unstereotyped reply:
18...♖e5!
In the game Magerramov-L.Guliev (Abu Dhabi 2002) White, after long thought, played
19.♘h3
Tempting is 19.♘xb4, but after 19...♕e7 20.♘xc6 bxc6 21.♘h3 ♕e6 White has nothing.
19...♘xd5 20.♕c1 ♘ce7 21.cxd5
And here by means of 21...♖c8! Black could have completely shut the white queen out of the game, obtaining a serious advantage. Instead, Black played
21...♖xd5

and after
22.♘f4 ♖xd1 23.♖xd1 ♕e8 24.♕d2 ♕b5 25.h3 ♘c6? 26.♕d5 ♕xd5 27.♖xd5 ♗h7 28.♖d7
White managed to activate his forces and complicate the game. It only remains to add that, having lost the thread of the game, and unable to assess the position objectively (continuing to play an equal position as if he had the advantage), Black eventually lost. At the same time, one cannot but praise White's calm play.

Conclusion: One must try to play in accordance with the demands of the position.

Loss of objectivity almost always spoils the game. – David Bronstein

Solution 176

Thanks to his outside passed pawn, Black is winning. This is not so hard to see. The main difficulty is not to get confused and keep calm enough to find the strongest continuation.
  A) **48...♗e6!**, trying to advance his main pawn, is the simplest and most convincing decision in this position: 49.b5 h3 50.♗h1 (50.♗f1 h2 51.♗g2 ♗d5−+) 50...♗d5

51.♗xd5 ♚xd5 52.b6 ♚c6 53.♚a6 h2 54.b7 h1♕ 55.b8♕ ♕a1#;

B) Although the continuation **48...♗d3** also wins, as is clear from the following variations: 49.b5 ♗xc2 (49...♚c5?! 50.b6) 50.♚b4 ♗a4 (it was also worth considering 50...♗xg6 51.♚c3 ♚c5 52.♚d2 ♗f5 or 52.b6 ♚xb6 53.♚d4 ♗f5 54.♚e5 h3 55.♗h1 g6).

However, in the game Potkin-L. Guliev (Linares 2002) Black was seriously engrossed in the analysis of the move 48...♗d3, but at the board, he did not see the move 50...♗a4 (only seen during home analysis) and, under the impression that all roads lead to Rome, decided to win the pawn in another, and, as it turns out, inferior way!

48...♗d5?!

The game continued:

49.♗f1 ♗e4 50.b5 ♚c7

50...♗xc2! 51.♚b4 ♗xg6 52.♚xc3 ♚c5−+.

51.♚b4 ♗f5

Finally Black returns to the correct path.

52.♚xc3 h3 53.♚d4 h2 54.♗g2

Black has lost many tempi and thanks to this, the game has become sharper. But the win has not yet been thrown away, although it has been made somewhat more difficult.

Black needs to make an intermediate bishop move with the aim of deflecting the white bishop from g2: 54...♗h3!! 55.♗h1 ♗c8 56.♚e3 ♗b7 57.♚f2 ♗xh1 58.♚g3 ♗e4−+.

In the game Black was too hasty! For this, he paid the price of a valuable half point, which he very much needed. There followed:

54...♗c8?

One mistake often leads to another. − Paul Keres

55.♚e3 ♗b7 56.♚f2

This is the difference!

56...h1♕ 57.♗xh1 ♗xh1

The position is still winning for Black, but in the game White managed to get a fortress:

58.♚e3 ♚d6 59.♚d4 ♗f3 60.c4 ♗h5? 61.c5+= ♚e6 62.c6? 62.♚e3!−+ ♚d6 63.♚e4 ♗xg6? 64.♚f4= ♗d3 65.♚g5 ♗e4 66.♚h5 ♚e7 67.♚g5

This is a fortress. As a result of a barely noticeable error (54...♗c8) we reach this beautiful and instructive position.

Small causes give birth to big consequences. − Alexander Alekhine

**67...⟨d6 68.⟨h5 ⟨f5 69.⟨g5 ⟨h7
70.⟨h5 ⟨c2 71.⟨g5 ⟨d3 72.⟨h5
⟨e7 73.b6 ⟨d6 74.b7 ⟨c7 75.⟨g5
⟨e4 ½-½**

Conclusion: Play the simpler way! Often in the endgame, the outcome depends on one tempo.

Simplicity is the most beautiful thing of all. (Japanese proverb)

Success is being in time. – Marina Svetaeva

Solution 177

White has a winning position. With the striking but fairly simple tactical blow **1.⟨xg7!** he could have obtained a decisive advantage. However, in the game S.Guliev-Sadigi (Teheran 2002) White sunk into long thought. He could not decide which move was better, 1.⟨xg7 or 1.⟨c7. In the end, he concluded that both moves were equally good and decided to avoid a sacrifice:
1.⟨c7?
But after the 'mirror' reply
1...⟨b7!
(the move White had overlooked)
2.⟨c3

(Black is favoured by 2.⟨xg7 ⟨xc7 3.⟨cxc7 f4!, so the queen must retreat)
2...⟨xa2
White found himself in a very difficult position.

Conclusion: *Enough is as good as a feast.* (English proverb)

The great danger is born at the moment of victory. – Napoleon

Solution 178

The position is very complicated and requires the ability to calculate variations. A close examination reveals that the bad positions of the white queen and bishop are of decisive importance. Black is winning.
1...f6!
A concrete tactical decision. At the same time, the following continuations only confuse the position:
  A) 1...exd4 2.⟨xd5 ⟨xc5 3.b4!;
  B) 1...h6 2.⟨g3 h5 3.dxe5!?;
  C) 1...⟨e7!? 2.⟨g3; or
  D) 1...e4 2.⟨g4 ⟨xg4 3.⟨xg4+ f5 4.⟨f4.
In the game Mallahi-S.Guliev (Meshxed 2002) there followed
2.⟨g3

(A) 2.♕xf6!? ♝e7 3.♕f7 (3.♕g7 e4
4.♘xd5 exf3 5.♘xe7+ (5.b4 ♕a3!)
5...♘xe7 6.♕xe7 ♖he8−+) 3...e4
4.♘xd5 exf3−+; or
 B) 2.♕h4!? h5! 3.♝xd5 g5! 4.♕g3
exd4 etc.)
2...h5!
(with the threat of 3...h4)
3.dxe5 h4! 4.♕f4 fxe5 5.b4 ♕xb4
and Black obtained a winning
position.

Conclusion: The usual scheme of
attack is for the foot-soldiers to go
first, the lower-ranking officers
behind them and only behind them
come the higher-ranking officers.

*The essence of a game should be
the search for truth, victory being a
demonstration of that truth. – Vasily
Smyslov*

Solution 179

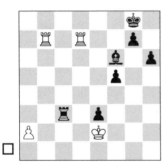

The material balance favours Black.
But the position is complicated
and requires a concrete-dynamic
assessment. In general, when
assessing positions with a non-
standard material balance, a non-
standard approach is needed. It
seems that the powerful white
rooks and his passed a-pawn should
decide the game.

In the game L.Guliev-Vera Gonzalez
(Linares 2002) Black failed to cope
with the complications over the
board and lost quickly.
39.♖dc7!
The exchange of a pair of rooks
favours White – this deprives
Black of the possibility of creating
counterplay.
39...♖a3?! 40.♖a7 ♖xa7 41.♖xa7 f4
A very interesting position. Rook
and rook's pawn on the queenside
face a bishop and four pawns on the
opposite flank. It is hard to believe
that Black will be forced to resign
within six moves.
42.a4 g5? 43.a5 g4 44.♖d7 ♝g5
44...g3 45.a6.
45.a6 f3+ 46.♔d3 f2 47.♔e2 1-0
Readers who are well acquainted
with the ending of rook vs pawn
will probably divine the secret of
the position. The endgame is equal!
Black should try to give the bishop
(ideally after the exchange of rooks)
for the a-pawn and then set up a
drawing fortress. Deep analysis
shows that this is possible. This
is how Black should play: 39...f4!
40.♖xc3 ♝xc3 41.a4 g5! 42.♖a7 ♔h8!
43.a5 ♝xa5 44.♖xa5 ♔g7,

analysis diagram

and we have a well-known
theoretical draw.

This is not the only way. The game continuation also holds the balance up to a certain moment, e.g. 42...♗c3 (instead of 42...g5?) 43.a5 ♗xa5 44.♖xa5 g5 (44...♔f7?? 45.♖f5+; 44...♔h7!? 45.♖a7 ♔g8, but not 45...♔g6? 46.♔f3!) 45.♖a7 ♔h8 46.♔f3 ♔g8.

Conclusion: It is essential to know as many theoretical endgame (and not only endgame!) positions as possible and head for them like a ship heading towards a lighthouse in bad weather!

With king and rook against king and four pawns, one can as a rule count only on a draw. – Alexander Panchenko

Solution 180

It seems at first glance that the position offers chances to both sides. The black king is extremely exposed and his pieces (especially the ♖e8 and the bishop) are in loose positions. But his strong attack on the long white diagonal compensates for the majority of the weaknesses in his position. However, White has at his disposal a surprising tactical possibility! His position is winning.

1.♕d7! ♕e4 (the only move) 2.♕xe8+ ♔g7 (2...♖f8 3.♕xe6+ and 4.f3) 3.♕e7+ ♔h8 4.♖a2!!. After this surprising move, the black attack fizzles out. In the variation 4...♖xg3+ 5.fxg3 ♕h1+ 6.♔f2 he has no chances.

In the game L.Guliev-Mamedyarov (Baku 2002) White missed 4.♖a2!! and avoided this continuation. Instead of this, he decided to win 'more solidly' and took the c-pawn. With opposite-coloured bishops and a closed structure this proved sufficient only for a draw. After the moves

1.♕xc4 ♗d5 2.♕a4?! (finally losing his remaining advantage)
2...♕xa4 3.♖xa4 ♖xc3 4.♗e3 ♖b8 5.♖a7 ♖cb3 6.♖d1 ♗e4

a draw was agreed. The move 4.♖a2!! was pointed out immediately after the game by Shakhriyar. Did you also see it?

Conclusion: The rook is a leisurely piece.

Paradox is the only truth. – George Bernard Shaw

Solution 181

I hope that the solution of this did not cost you too much time. In the game Kallio-L.Guliev (Linares 2002) Black exploited the weakness of the white king and the activity of his pieces in the centre to land a tactical blow:

32...♖xc4+! 33.♔b1

He also loses after 33.♕xc4 ♗h6+ 34.♔d1 (34.♖e3 ♕xf2) 34...♕b1+ 35.♔e2 ♕xb2+ with a mating attack.

33...♕xd3+ 34.♖xd3 ♖xa4 35.♖d2 ♔f7 36.♘xc7 ♖d4 37.♖c2 ♖f5 38.♖g3 e4

And Black was left with two extra pawns, which he soon realised.

Conclusion: Combinations are not always deeply hidden from one's eyes.

Learn from all, imitate nobody. – Maxim Gorky

Solution 182

White's advantage is not in doubt. With his last move (37...♕f8?) Black allowed a tactical solution to the position. In the game L.Guliev-Gyimesi (Linares 2002) White did see the gift offered to him:

38.♖xe6! ♖f5

Hopeless is 38...fxe6 39.♖h8+ ♔xh8 40.♕xf8+.

39.d5!

Maybe this is what Black had missed.

39...fxe6 40.♖h8+ ♔f7 41.♖xf8+ ♔xf8 42.♕h6+ ♔e7 43.♕g7+ ♔d6 44.♕xg6 ♖xd5 45.h4 ♖f5 46.h5

And after a few moves, White won.

Conclusion: A weakness on the long diagonal is almost always the source of a combinational motif!

'Divide and rule' is a wise rule, but 'unite and direct' is even better. – Johann Wolfgang von Goethe

Solution 183

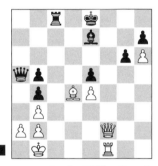

In the game De la Villa Garcia-L. Guliev (Linares 2002), exploiting his opponent's uncertain play after coming out of the opening, Black seized the initiative. White decided to complicate play with a piece sacrifice, at the same time opening the game and exploiting the fact that the black king is in the centre. It appears that Black's position is superior. In order to be convinced that in fact it is equal, both sides must find a series of accurate moves.

36...♕a8!

The queen returns, so as actively to oppose the white centre. In the game he reacted badly and after

37.♗b6 ♕xe4+ 38.♔a1 ♕f4 39.♕e1 ♕xh6 40.♗a5

(40.♕xe5 ♖c1+)

40...♕g5 41.♔b1 ♕g2 42.♗xb4 ♖c2 43.♗c3 ♖e2 44.♕c1 b4! 45.♗xb4 ♖c2!

resigned. For a long time the authors were convinced that the game had ended logically. However, when the position was entered into the computer, they were greatly surprised. White has a beautiful way to draw!:

37.♕f7+ ♔d7 (37...♔d8? 38.♗b6+ ♔d7 39.♖d1+ and White soon mates) 38.♗c3!! ♕xe4+ 39.♔a1 (39.♔c1?? ♕e3+ 40.♔b1 ♕d3+ and 41...bxc3–+ next) 39...bxc3 40.♖d1+ ♔c6 41.♕e6+ ♔b7 42.♖d7+! ♖c7 43.♖xc7+ ♔xc7 44.♕xe7+ ♔b6 45.♕d8+ and White gives perpetual check.

Conclusion: The road to the centre is not always direct!

I think the scientists lied. The hole in their theory: development goes not in a spiral, but at random. – Vladimir Vysotsky

Solution 184

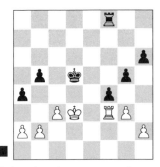

Black is winning. Do you know the Saavedra study (1895)?

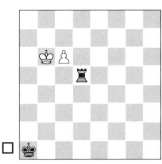

1.c7 ♖d6+ 2.♔b5 ♖d5+ 3.♔b4 ♖d4+ 4.♔b3 ♖d3+ 5.♔c2 ♖d4 6.c8♖ ♖a4 7.♔b3+−

Or the famous game Ortueta-Sanz (Madrid 1934)?

30...♖d2 31.♘a4 ♖xb2!! 32.♘xb2 c3! 33.♖xb6 c4!! 34.♖b4 a5 35.♘xc4 c2 0-1

If you know these classic examples, then the solution here will not cause you much trouble:

1...fxg3! 2.♖xf8

More tenacious was 2.♖xg3 ♖f2 3.♖h3! ♖xb2 4.♖xh6 ♖xa2 5.♖h5 (5.h4!) 5...♖g2 6.h4 ♖g3+ 7.♔d2 (7.♔c2 ♔c4) 7...♔c4 8.♖xg5 ♖d3+ 9.♔e2 ♖d8, although here Black's win is only a question of time.

2...g2

In the game Tadzhik-S.Guliev (Teheran 2002) Black won.

Conclusion: Beware of discovered attacks!

Everything is new that is well forgotten. (proverb)

Solution 185

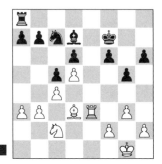

Black has prospects of creating active play on the queenside. In combination with the 'good' bishop, this allows us to assess the position as somewhat better for Black.
The best way to underline this assessment is with the precise **29... b5!**, planning ...bxc4, bxc4 ...♖b8.
At the board, Black did not like 30.b4!?, although even here, after 30...bxc4 31.♗xc4 cxb4 32.♘xb4 a5! 33.♘c6 ♗xc6 34.dxc6+ d5 35.♗f1 (35.♗a2 ♖b8!) 35...♖b8! and then ...♖b6 Black is better, thanks to the weakness of the c6-pawn.
But in the game Delaney-S.Guliev (Cappelle-la-Grande 2003) Black decided that queenside play could wait and that he should first improve his position on the kingside:
29...f5??
And after
30.♖f3!
(this Black had missed)
30...f4
(there is nothing else)

31.gxf4 g4 32.♖g3 h5 33.♘e3
he found himself in a difficult position.
In case of **29...♖e8** the game is simplified and completely equalised.

Conclusion: More haste, less speed!

Life hurries if we ourselves dawdle. – Daniil Granin

Solution 186

White is better, as is not hard to see from the structure. However, the ♘h3 is out of play. This gives Black the chance to obtain counterplay. 23...e5? 24.dxe6 (24.♘f2!?) 24...♖xe6 25.♖xe6 ♘xe6 26.♕xd6! favours White. Black's position is also not very cheerful after 23...♕h5 24.♔g2 ♖ef8 25.g4!?.
In the game Andersson-S.Guliev (Istanbul 2003) Black played:
23...♗xc3
He was counting on the replies 24.♕xc3 or 24.♖xc3 and then playing ...e7-e5, getting rid of the weakness on e7. For example: 24.♖xc3 e5 25.dxe6 ♖xe6 26.♖xe6 ♕xe6 or 24.♕xc3 e5 25.dxe6 ♖xe6, and in both cases the d6-pawn is not under attack. However, White's reply

24.bxc3!!
left him in a state of shock. After
24...♖ef8 25.♔g2 ♕h7 26.f4!
White's advantage had only
increased.
Evidently, Black should have
tried **24...e5!?**, and in the event
of 25.dxe6 ♖xe6 26.♖xe6 ♘xe6
27.♕xd6 ♘f8 28.♕xg6+ ♘xg6
29.♔g2 ♖d7, thanks to the offside
knight on h3 and the weakness
of the queenside pawns, he has
sufficient counterplay.

Conclusion: As we see, doubled
pawns are not always weak pawns!

*No, this seemingly strange strategic
tandem (vertical phalanx) still has a lot
of unsolved and undescribed properties.
It is no wonder that one time, in answer
to the question 'What is your favourite
piece?', Grandmaster David Bronstein
quite seriously answered: 'A doubled
pawn!' – Igor Zaitsev*

Solution 187

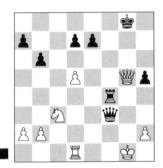

What a simple question, you are
probably thinking. Hopefully, you
all saw that
32...♔f7??
is a terrible blunder. After
33.♕xf4+

Black has to resign, since after the
recapture there follows 34.♖f1.
But do not be surprised – this
is precisely what happened in
the game Kacheishvili-S.Guliev
(Istanbul 2003).
The correct reply is **32...♔h7!**
(nothing comes from 32...♔h8
33.♕e5+) **33.♕xe7+ ♔h6!** (not
33...♔g6 34.♕d6+) **34.♕xd7 ♕e3+
35.♔h1 ♖f6! 36.♕c6** (the only
move) **36...♕f3+ 37.♔g1 ♕f2+!
38.♔h1 ♖xc6 39.dxc6 h4!** with a
decisive advantage to Black.

Conclusion: One must think about
where such elementary oversights
come from?

*The most difficult thing is to make
demands on yourself. – Anton
Makarenko*

Solution 188

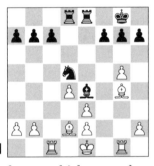

White has two bishops and an
extra pawn. However, thanks to
the blockading pieces in the centre
and their supporting rooks, Black
controls the whole board. These
factors amount to a clear advantage
for Black.
By playing **19...♖d6!**, Black could
have increased his superiority. It is
not easy for White to defend against

the threats on the queenside, e.g. 20.h4 ♖a6 21.a3 (21.a4!?) 21...♖b6 22.b4 ♖a6 23.♖a1 ♖e7 followed by ...♘d5-b6-c4.

But in the game S.Guliev-Etchegaray (Cappelle-la-Grande 2003) there followed the stereotyped:

19...c6? 20.h4 f5?

Up to here the game was equal. Black should not have opened the game (and it is not obvious what White can do). But after the incautious text move the position opens up and the white bishops begin to take over:

21.gxf6 ♘xf6 22.♗f3 ♗xf3?

22...♖d5!.

23.exf3 ♖xd4 24.e4!

And already it is White who is better.

Conclusion: The two bishops are not necessary an advantage in themselves, but are a source of problems for the opponent.

When you let yourself be tamed, it ends in tears. – Antoine de Saint-Exupéry

Solution 189

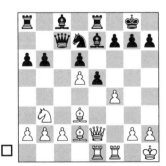

Due to inaccurate handling of the opening, Black has an unpleasant position. He has fallen under a

typical Sicilian attack. In the game L.Guliev-Gara (Condom 2003) White quickly decided the game in his favour with a few well-calculated tactical blows.

16.fxe5! ♘xe5 17.♗xh7+! ♔xh7 18.♕h5+ ♔g8 19.♖xe5 g6 20.♕f3 ♖f8 21.♖ee1 ♖a7 22.♘d4 ♗b7 23.♗h6 ♕c4 24.♖xe7 ♗xd5 25.♕f6

And Black resigned.

Conclusion: What are the first principles of opening play?

Correct play in the opening is a great art. To master it, you must always remember the basic opening principle that for the successful implementation of any plan, one needs sensible mobilisation of the forces. – Alexey Suetin

Solution 190

Control of the a-file, the strong centralized knight and the weak squares in the black camp all add up to a large advantage to White. But if you examine the position more closely, you will see that White in fact has a winning attack.

In the game L.Guliev-Pinter (Condom 2003) the coordinated action of the white pieces quickly decided the game:

41.♖a7! ♖f7

41...♖e7 42.♘c6; 41...♕xa7 42.♘e6+.

42.♖xd7! ♖xd7 43.♖xf6 ♘f7 44.♗d1!
A timely use of a typical manoeuvre.

44...♕d8 45.♘e6+ ♖xe6 46.♖xe6 ♘e5 47.♗h5 ♘g6 48.♕f5
Also sufficient for a win was 48.♗xg6 hxg6 49.♕d4+ ♔h7 50.♕f6 ♕xf6 51.♖xf6, but the queen manoeuvre used in the game is more attractive.

48...♘h4
Or 48...♖f7 49.♖xg6+ hxg6 50.♕xg6+.

49.♕g4 ♖a7 50.♕d1 ♕b6 51.♕f1 ♕d8 52.♖e8
And Black resigned because of 52...♕f6 53.♖g8+.

Conclusion: In which opening do you feel like a fish in water?

... back in his day, Capablanca considered the Spanish to be the touchstone of positional understanding. – Anatoly Karpov

Solution 191

The move
29.♗xd5
is mistaken and leads to White's defeat. A quick transfer of the queen and rook to the kingside in the game Aout-L.Guliev (Condom 2003)

placed White in an impossible position:

29...♖h4! 30.♖f3 ♗xd5 31.♖xf5?
31.♕xd5=.

31...♕g6
The threat is 32...♕g3.

32.♖f3 ♗xf3 33.gxf3 ♖e8 34.♘c5 ♕f5 35.♘d3 ♖e6
And within a few moves Black won.

Conclusion: Why do you think White missed the move 29...♖h4 ?

Don't dig a pit for someone else, lest you fall into it yourself. (proverb)

Solution 192

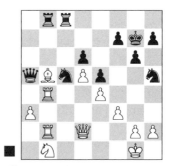

26...♕a7! 27.♔h1
Interestingly, after 27.♔f1 and even 27.♕f2 Black's attacking method would not change.

27...♖xb5! 28.♖xb5 ♘d3 29.♘c3 ♕d4! 30.♘a2
He is not saved by either 30.♘d1 ♖c1, or 30.♖b1 ♖xc3.

30...♘hf4 31.g3? ♘f2+ 32.♕xf2 ♕d1+ 33.♕g1 ♕xf3+ 34.♖g2 ♖c2
And White resigned. This is how Black finished off his attack in the game Dumitrache-L.Guliev (La Fère 2003).
It seems to the authors that this combination is one of the loveliest in the book.

Conclusion: Diagonals are no less important than ranks and files!

White brought off a typical attack: first he pinned the opponent's forces down on the queenside, and then he transferred the centre of gravity of the fight to the opposite side of the board at the right time. To do this, he had to sacrifice the exchange, but he obtained an advantage in force at the site of the decisive battle.

Thus wrote Efim Geller, describing the game Geller-Antoshin (Moscow 1970). These words could equally apply to Black's play in the above example!

Solution 193

In the game Chuchelov-S.Guliev (Istanbul 2003) after the moves
26...♖xc1? 27.♕xc1 ♖c8?! 28.♘c6! ♗f6?! 29.a4! bxa4 30.b4
White obtained a large advantage and later won.
However, by means of **26...f4!**
Black could have organised a strong attack on the position of the white king. The following variations show how dangerous it could be: 27.exf4 gxf4 28.gxf4 ♗d4 (28...♕xf4!? 29.♘f3 ♗c3 30.♖xe7 ♗d4! or 30.♖f1 ♘e5 with a very complicated game)
 A) 29.♘e4 ♕xf4!;

B) 29.♖f1 ♕xf4 30.♘f3 ♗xf2+!−+;
 C) 29.♘d3 ♖xc1 30.♕xc1 ♖c8!
(30...♕h7? 31.♕c7!) 31.♕d1 ♕h7
32.♘f1 ♖c3! and Black's initiative is very threatening.
Over the board, Black thought a good deal about the break ...f5-f4, but just at the key moment, he unfortunately forgot about it! The possibility was pointed out in the post-mortem by the well-known grandmaster Viktor Kupreichik.

Conclusion: *Every dog has his day.* (proverb)

When too much energy is spent on promises, too little remains to fulfil them. – Konstantin Simonov

Solution 194

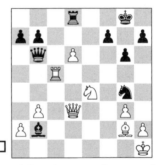

The position is very sharp and complicated. Here we need the ability to calculate numerous variations and have excellent attacking imagination. In the game S.Guliev-Bacrot (Istanbul 2003) White, in time trouble, chose
31.h3??
And now:
31...♘f2+
Even stronger was 31...♕xc5!.
32.♘xf2 ♕xc5 33.♘e4 ♕d4
33...♕b6!?.

34.♕c2 ♗a3 35.♕c7

35...♖f8

Black is promised a large advantage after 35...♖xd6!.

36.h4 h6 37.d7 ♗e7 38.♘c3 ♗d8 39.♕c8 ♗b6 40.♔h2 ♕g1+ 41.♔h3 ♕e3 42.♘d5 ♕e6+ 43.♔h2 ♖d8 44.♕c3 ♖xd7 45.♘f6+ ♔f8 46.♘xd7+ ♕xd7 47.♕h8+ ♔e7 48.♕xh6

And, having passed the control, and with the help of his opponent, White made a draw.

However, the diagram position is roughly equal. This can be confirmed in two ways:

A) **31.♕c4!? ♘e3 32.♕d3** (no other possibilities for White are apparent, e.g. 32.♕e2 ♗d4 etc.) **32...♘g4** with a repetition of moves;

B) **31.♕c2 ♘f6** (after 31...♗a3? 32.♖c8 ♖xc8 33.♕xc8+ ♔g7 34.♕xg4 f5 35.♕d1! White has the advantage) **32.♖c8 ♘xe4 33.♖xd8+ ♕xd8 34.♗xe4 ♗e5 35.♗xb7 ♕xd6=.**

Time trouble is a secret world, which produces miracles. One player gets to laugh at the mistakes that result, while the other cries!

Conclusion: A feeling for time is important in a chess player.

If you are in time trouble, then it's better to play 'solidly'. Before the onset of time trouble, you must make moves faster. In the opponent's time pressure, do not succumb to the pace of his game, because he is internally ready to make moves quickly, but you are not. The chances of an error in this situation are much higher for you. In the opponent's time trouble, make moves in batches (2-3-4). In any case, you need strong nerves. – Alexander Panchenko

Solution 195

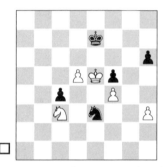

This appears to be a very simple position, but the more one looks at it, the more one realises that it is not so easy.

The game S.Guliev-Erdogu (Istanbul 2003) after the moves

56.♔d4? ♘g2 57.♘e2 ♔d6 58.♘g3 ♘xf4 59.♘xf5+ ♔d7 60.h4 c3 61.♔xc3 ♘xd5+ 62.♔d4 ♘e7 63.♘xh6 ♘g6

ended in a draw.

A) The apparently very strong 56.♘a4 also gives nothing after 56...♘d1! 57.d6+ ♔d8! 58.♔e6 c3 59.♘c5 c2 and Black has sufficient counterplay;

B) No better was 56.♘b5 ♔d7 57.d6 ♘d1! 58.♔d4 c3 59.♔d3 ♘f2+=;

C) However, White can win by energetic play: **56.d6+! ♔d7 57.♘a4!**

c3!? 58.♘xc3 ♘c4+ 59.♔xf5 ♘xd6+ 60.♔f6+–.

Conclusion: An attack on the king is even possible in a simple endgame.

In life there is nothing better than one's own experience. – Walter Scott

Solution 196

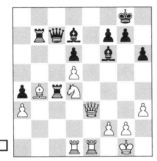

The black pieces, especially his rooks, clearly lack harmony. His kingside lacks the support of the major pieces. Thanks to all of this, White has a large advantage. Black has nothing with which to oppose his opponent's powerful initiative. The game L.Guliev-Kaiumov (Teheran 2003) continued:
33.♘c6!
White has created numerous threats (e.g. 34.♘a5 or 34.♕d3), so Black must take the knight.
33...♗xc6 34.dxc6 ♕xc6
Or 34...♖xc6 35.♕e8+ ♔h7 36.♗xd6 ♕c8 (36...♖xd6 37.♖xd6 ♕xd6 38.♕e4+ g6 39.♕xb7) 37.♕e4+ g6 38.♕xa4.
35.♖xd6 ♕b5 36.♖xf6!
The undefended position of the black king starts to have its say.
36...gxf6 37.♕xh6 ♖xb4 38.axb4 f5 39.♖c1 ♖e7 40.♕g5+ ♔f8 41.♕f6 ♖e6 42.♕h8+ ♔e7 43.♖c7+ 1-0

Conclusion: Sometimes one suspects that the chess pieces have a better feeling of harmony than humans!

Character is power over yourself, talent power over others. – Vasily Kluchevsky

Solution 197

White has a clear advantage. The knight on f5 is frequently a harbinger of an attack on the enemy king's castled position. In this case the f5-square fulfils the function of an outpost. So as to clear the path for the rooks and queen to join in the attack, White in the game S.Guliev-Ravi (Kish 2003) sacrificed a pawn:
30.h4!
The ♗g5 prevents White's attack.
30...♗xh4
Or 30...♗e7 31.♘xh6+ gxh6 32.♕g6+ ♘g7 33.♖f7! ♖xf7 34.♖xf7 ♗f8 35.g5! (35.e6? ♕xh4+) 35...hxg5 (35...h5 36.e6) 36.e6 g4 37.♗f2 (37. e7 ♕xe7 38.♖xe7 ♗xe7 39.♕xg4+–) 37...♘b6 38.h5 and h5-h6, with a decisive advantage.
31.♘xh6+! gxh6
31...♔h8 32.♖xf8+ ♘dxf8 33.♘f7+.
32.♕g6+ ♘g7 33.♖f7 ♖xf7 34.♖xf7 ♕f8 35.e6 ♗g5 36.♗h2 ♘f6 37.♗d6
And Black resigned.

Conclusion: Try to place your knights on the fifth rank whilst keeping the enemy's knights away from there!

A knight which reaches the fifth rank, as a rule, offers good attacking chances. Such a knight is usually stronger than a bishop. – Max Euwe, Haije Kramer

Solution 198

One is struck by the passivity of the black pieces. However, one should not always believe one's first impression. Sometimes this happens during the retreat phase of a regrouping. The weakened position of the king, the pawn minus and the insufficiently prepared activity by the white pieces renders White's position hopeless.
In the game Ettekhadi-L.Guliev (Teheran 2003) Black decided to reply to White's kingside play with a blow in the centre! In general, this is a common situation, but here the white pawn gets the chance to advance. Therefore, exact calculation is required.
There followed
1...d5! 2.e5 g5!
(this move is the point of Black's combination)
3.♕h6 gxf4 4.exf6

(now there is a terrible threat of 5.♕xf8+!)
4...♖g8
(also good is 4...♗xf6)
5.♖e2 ♖g6 6.♖xe6 ♔g8!
(but not 6...♕xe6? 7.f7+ or 6...♖xh6? 7.♖e8+)
and Black won.

Conclusion: Retreat is not always cowardice, sometimes it is cunning.

Drawing the enemy forces forward and counterattacking at the weakest spot is one of the most tried and tested devices in chess. – Viktor Golenishchev

Solution 199

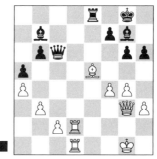

This very complicated position, strangely, is equal! White has a material advantage, but his strong play on the h1-a8 diagonal and exposed white king compensate for this: **32...♖xe5! 33.fxe5 ♗xe5 34.♕e3** (34.♕xe5 ♕h1+ 35.♔f2 ♕f3+ 36.♔e1 ♕h1+=) **34...♗d4!** (34...♕h1+ 35.♔f2 ♕g2+ 36.♔e1 ♕h1+ 37.♔e2 ♕g2+ 38.♕f2 ♕e4+ 39.♕e3 ♕g2+ 40.♔d3 ♕d5+ also led to a draw) **35.♕xd4 ♕h1+ 36.♔f2 ♕f3+ 37.♔e1 ♕h1+=.**
One of those lovely examples, where the strength of two bishops is crystal clear. On the chessboard,

diagonals are no less important than ranks and files!

In the game Moradiabadi-L.Guliev (Teheran 2003) Black saw this possibility, but it seemed to him that his position was better and he had the right to count on more than a draw. After the moves

32...♗f8? 33.♔h2! ♗e7? 34.♕c3! ♕e6 35.♕c4 ♕xc4 bxc4

he realised his mistake and soon had to resign.

Conclusion: Overrating possibilities, both yours and your opponent's, is a serious weakness.

If a person knows the means, he knows everything. – Thomas Carlyle

Solution 200

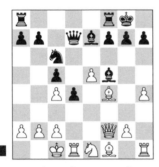

Even a passing glance at the position is enough to reveal that Black is well ahead in development. Therefore opening the game favours him. In the game Mallahi-S.Guliev (Kish 2003) Black underlined all the advantages of his position by means of:

13...f6!
After
14.exf6 ♗xf6
(14...♖xf6!?)
15.♗d3 ♗e5 16.g3 ♖ae8

Black's advantage became obvious, as he is dictating the course of the game.

Conclusion: If you have an advantage in development, try to open the position.

If you have strength, then you must attack; if not, the advantage will be hidden and not show itself. – Emanuel Lasker

Solution 201

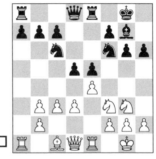

The position is absolutely equal. Black is active in the centre, but the white position has no serious defects. The ♖a1 and ♗c1, even in their original positions, fulfil some functions. White should play **13.b4!**, getting rid of the backward pawn, and then continue play in quiet style, e.g. h2-h3, ♕c2 (or ♕b3). This would maintain equality.

But in the game Moradiabadi-S. Guliev (Kish 2003) White momentarily forgot about the compromised position of the b3-pawn and carelessly played:

13.♕e2?!
Black's reply
13...a5!
disturbed his equanimity, and without any justification, he

187

launched a pawn storm on the kingside:

14.h4?!

By means of 14.♕c2 and then ♗e3 White could successfully defend, since his position is not really much worse.

14...h5! 15.♗g5 ♕d7 16.♖ad1 ♘g4! 17.♘h2 ♘xh2 18.♔xh2 d4!? 19.f3?! b5!

Black already has a large advantage. **20.♕c2 dxc3 21.bxc3 a4 22.♖a1 ♘d8! 23.bxa4 bxa4 24.♖a2 ♖e6 25.♘e2 ♖d6 26.♖ea1 ♖da6! 27.♗xd8 ♕xd8 28.g3 a3!**

And Black soon won.

Conclusion: Don't mess with backward pawns!

A backward pawn can be a serious defect in a pawn structure, especially if it is on a half-open file and the square in front of it is under enemy control. – Viktor Golenishchev

In our example, we see that such a pawn can be a serious problem, when not on a half-open file.

Solution 202

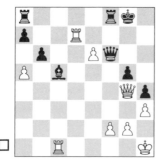

White is winning:

35.♖xc5!

35.♖d5? ♗e7!.

35...bxc5 36.♖d5 ♖fe8 37.♖xg5+ ♔f8 38.♖f5 ♔e7 39.♖xf6 ♔xf6 40.♕xh4+ ♔xe6 41.♕c4+ ♔d6 42.f4 ♖e1+ 43.♔h2 ♖ae8 44.f5 ♖8e4 45.♕d3+ ♔e5 46.♕c3+ ♔d5 47.f6

And in a few more moves, Black resigned in the game L.Guliev-Darban (Isfahan 2004).

Conclusion: In dynamic positions, as in many others, the initiative plays a principal role!

Growing space and an increasing tempo are two reliable indications of the fact that the position has begun to live according to the laws of dynamics, rather than statics. – Igor Zaitsev

Solution 203

Apart from the bishop on e2, all of White's pieces are pointing at the d5-pawn and it is not obvious how to defend it. It seems that Black must accept its loss. However, tactics come to the rescue. Black has available a tactical resource, which immediately takes the game into drawing channels. In the game Kim-S.Guliev (Moscow 2004) Black did not miss his chance. The position is equal.

1...c4! 2.♘xd5+ ♗xd5 3.♖xd5 cxb3 4.axb3 ♗xc3 5.♗c4 ♖xd5

And now the players agreed a draw, on account of the following variations: 6.♖xd5 ♖d8 7.♖xd8 (the line 7.♖h5 ♖d1+ 8.♗f1 ♗d4 9.♖xh6 ♖d2! actually favours Black) 7...♔xd8 8.♗xf7 ♔e7=.

In the Azeri folk epic Koroghlu, it is told that at one point, the eponymous hero was surrounded in the city of Kars. Until evening, he somehow held out against the superior forces of the enemy, but at night, given the superiority of the enemy in numbers, he told his soldiers the famous words:

There are ten types of bravery, nine of which involve running away.

... and gave the command to flee, using the darkness! In this position, Black followed this principle.

Conclusion: The main thing is to understand in time that the position is dangerous and to take measures to hold the balance.

... the hardest thing in chess is to correctly and justifiably, at just the right time, sacrifice a pawn. – Alexander Kotov

Solution 204

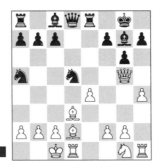

Here in the game Kurenkov-S. Guliev (Moscow 2004) Black thought for a long time. The continuation 1...♕xg5 2.hxg5 ♘c3 3.♗xc3 ♗xc3 4.bxc3 favours White. It was worth considering 1...♕f6 2.♕xf6 ♘xf6 3.♗xa5 b6! 4.♗c3 (4.♗b5 bxa5 5.♗xe8 ♘xe8 6.♖d8 ♔f8!∓) 4...♘xe4 5.♗xe4 ♖xe4 6.♖d8+ ♗f8 7.♘f3 ♗b7∓. However, he decided to choose a sharp and risky path, where he would manage to organise a counterattack:

1...♘c6 2.exd5

Stronger was 2.♕xd5 ♕f6! 3.♗c3 ♕f4+ 4.♔b1 (or 4.♗d2 ♕xf2 5.♗c3 with a repetition of moves) 4...♗xc3 5.♘e2 ♕xf2 6.♖df1 ♘b4 7.♕c4 ♘xd3 with a complicated and roughly equal game.

2...♘e5 3.♗b5

3.♕xd8 ♘xd3+ 4.cxd3 ♖xd8 is favourable for Black.

3...♕xd5 4.♗xe8

4...♕xa2?!

Now the computer considers the game equal. From its point of view, there was an advantage after 4...♗g4!, but, objectively speaking, even after the text move, it is not easy for White to defend against the numerous threats.

5.♗c3

On 5.♗b4 a possibility is 5...♗g4
6.♗xf7+ (6.♖d8 ♕a1+ 7.♔d2 ♕d1+;
6.f3 ♖xe8 7.♖d8 ♕a1+ 8.♔d2
♘c4+ 9.♔d3 ♘xb2+ 10.♔d2 ♕e1#)
6...♘xf7 7.♕xg4 ♗h6+ 8.f4 ♘e5
9.♕g3 ♘c4.

5...♗g4

6.♖e1??

Now Black gets an irresistible
attack.

A) Also bad is 6.♖d8 ♕a1+ 7.♔d2
♕d1+; or

B) 6.f3 ♖xe8 7.♖d8 (7.fxg4 ♘c4)
7...♕a1+ 8.♔d2 ♘c4+ 9.♔d3 ♕f1+;

C) However, White had at his
disposal an adequate defence,
and not only one. For example:
6.♗xf7+ ♔xf7! (6...♘xf7 7.♕xg4
favours White) 7.♘f3! ♗xf3 8.♗xe5
(8.gxf3? ♗f6! 9.♕h6 ♕a1+ 10.♔d2
♖d8+−+) 8...♗xd1 (also possible is
8...♕a1+ 9.♔d2 ♕a5+ 10.c3 (10.♔e3
♗xd1 11.♕f4+ ♔g8 12.♕c4+ ♔h8
13.♗xg7+ ♔xg7 14.♕d4+ with
equality) 10...♗xd1 11.♕f4+ ♔g8
12.♕c4+ ♔h8 13.♗xg7+ ♔xg7
14.♖xd1=) 9.♗xg7 ♔xg7 10.♕e5+
♔g8 11.♖xd1 ♕a1+ 12.♔d2 ♖d8+
13.♔c3 and after any capture on d1,
White has perpetual check;

D) Also possible is 6.♘f3 ♗xf3
7.♗xe5! (7.gxf3?! ♖xe8 (7...♘c4
♗xf7+ ♔xf7 9.♖d7++− , but it was
worth considering 7...f6!?) 8.♗xe5

(8.♖d8 ♕a1+ 9.♔d2 ♘xf3+ 10.♔d3
♕a6+−+) 8...♗xe5 − Black has
more than sufficient play for the
exchange and his chances are
preferable) 7...♕a1+ 8.♔d2 ♕a5+
9.♔c1 ♕a1+: evidently, the sides
must settle for a repetition.

6...f6!

Also good was 6...♖xe8.

7.♕f4 ♖d8!

Here too, the capture on e8 was
possible, but Black chooses to attack.

8.b3 ♗f8! 9.b4

9.♗b2 ♗a3 and mate is unstoppable.

9...♗f5

9...♘c4?? 10.♗f7+!! ♔xf7 11.♕xf6+
♔g8 12.♕h8+ ♔f7 13.♕xh7++−.

10.♗b2 ♘c4 11.♕xc4+ ♕xc4

And soon Black won.

Conclusion: Sometimes our
thoughts and actions do not
correspond.

*His 'developed' pieces cannot show their
attacking potential, and in defence, are
quite useless! – Hans Kmoch*

Solution 205

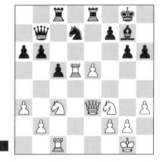

The e5-pawn is cut off from the
main part of its forces. Its defence
causes White difficulties, which
means that the assessment of
the position is that Black has the

advantage. With **1...♛c7!** Black could have forced the reply 2.♜e1 and then, by playing ...♜e7 and ...♜ce8, placed serious difficulties before White.
In the game S.Guliev-Kharitonov (Serpukhov 2004) Black rushed and immediately played:
1...♜e7?
1...♞f8 2.♜cd1 ♞e6 3.♞e4! is also better for White.
2.♜cd1 ♜ce8

And now there followed:
3.e6! ♞f6
After 3...fxe6 4.♜d6! White has strong compensation for the pawn, whilst in the event of 3...♜xe6 4.♜xd7 he simply has an extra piece.
4.exf7+ ♜xf7 5.♜d8 ♜ff8 6.♜xe8 ♜xe8 7.♛d3 g5 8.♛c4+ ♚h8 9.♜d6 ♛c7 10.♛d3
And White has a large advantage.

Conclusion: How does one determine when one needs to be patient and when to hurry?

The main principle of conducting an attack is that the object of the attack should most of all be immobile. – Aron Nimzowitsch

In this example, Black forgot that the object of attack (the e5-pawn) was mobile!

Solution 206

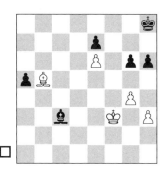

The position is drawn. Black's plan is to play ...♝e1, preventing the advance of the white pawns, and then to bring his king on the route ...♚h8-g7-f6-e5 (g5), creating pressure on Black's position. The a5-pawn is ready at any moment to advance, deflecting the white pieces. All of these factors indicate that White's defence is not easy. If the black king gets to e5, it will be very hard to save White's position. He has two possibilities:
A) Passive defence: 1.♝e8 ♚g7 2.♚e4 ♚f6 3.♚d5 ♝e1 4.♝d7 ♚g5 5.♝e8 ♚h4 6.♝xg6 ♚xh3 7.♝h5! (the only move; bad is 7.♝f5? ♚g3 and then ...♚f4-g5 and ...h6-h5−+). Now White's plan is to transfer the king to a4 or a2, while the bishop defends on the h5-e8 diagonal. If Black attacks the e6-pawn, then we reply ♝f7, whilst if he goes after the g4-pawn, there follows ♝h5 etc.: 7...a4 8.♚c4 ♚g3 9.♚d3! and then ♚c2-b3-a2=;
B) White, by advancing the h-pawn to the h5-square, prepares to carry out the plan described above. However, along the way there is a trap.

In the game S.Guliev-Abdullazanov (Serpukhov 2004) Black fell into this trap.

1.h4 ♔g7?

Now the trap springs. Black missed the principal continuation, but as the following variations show, there White holds equality: 1...♗e1! 2.h5 gxh5 3.gxh5 ♔g7 4.♔e4 ♔f6 5.♔d5 (5.♗d7!?) 5...♗g3 6.♗d7, and then the white king goes to a4 and as soon as the black king attacks the h5-pawn, there follows ♗e8 and it is not obvious how Black can make progress.

2.g5!

This is the trap – the black king is shut in.

2...♗d2 3.♔g4 ♗c1 4.♗a4

And the king cannot escape the corner. The players agreed a draw.

Conclusion: Not only birds, but also kings, can end up in cages!

Building a fortress is an important and frequently-seen method of defending in the endgame. – Mark Dvoretsky

Solution 207

White has a space advantage. Therefore it seems to the 'naked eye' that he has a serious advantage. However, Black's pieces are well developed, and the small defects in his pawn structure are not really felt. In the game Khrushulev-S.Guliev (Serpukhov 2004) there followed:

1.♕d3? ♘xd5 2.exd5 ♖xe1+ 3.♖xe1 ♗xb2 4.♘xb2 ♕g5!

And White had serious problems. There followed:

5.c4

5.♖d1 ♖e8 6.♘c4? ♗xd5! 7.♕xd5? ♖e1+ 8.♔h2 ♕f4+ favours Black.

5...c6! 6.dxc6

If 6.♖d1, then 6...♖e8, threatening 7...cxd5 and 8...♖e5!, after which the d5-pawn is in danger.

6...♗xc6 7.♕g3 ♕xg3 8.fxg3 ♔f8 9.♔f2 a5 10.♖d1 ♔e7 11.♖d3 a4

And Black's advantage became real. White should have gone **1.♘xf6+ ♗xf6 2.♗xf6 ♖xf6** (2...♕xf6?! 3.♕xf6 ♖xf6 4.e5±) **3.♕g3!** followed by e4-e5 and f2-f4, after which he has the better chances.

1.♘c3? would be a serious mistake because of 1...♘xe4!. This was a 'distraction' question.

Conclusion: Placing the pieces nicely in the centre is not a guarantee of an advantage!

60 days a year I play in tournaments, 5 days I rest and 300 I work on my game. – Akiba Rubinstein

Solution 208

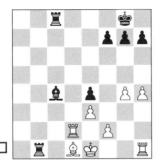

The game is equal. A tactic saves White, who is almost completely stalemated:

26.f3! exf3 27.♔f2 ♗e2 28.♖e1 ♗xd1

And here in the game S.Guliev-Khairullin (Moscow 2004) the players agreed a draw.

Conclusion: Even the great Steinitz, all those years ago, said that one could get away with not castling!

Strategy requires reflection, tactics a penetrating glance. – Max Euwe

Solution 209

Having sacrificed the exchange, White has obtained a powerful bishop and the possibility of creating connected passed pawns on the queenside. The most important thing in the position is the lack of open lines, which makes it hard for the black rooks to work effectively. In the game S.Guliev-Maletin (Moscow 2004), with the move

28.d5!

White increased his advantage.

28...f4

In the event of 28...cxd5 29.♕d4 White, by playing ♗e5, will be able in comfort to play b4-b5; it is also worth considering the immediate 29.b5!?.

29.dxc6 fxg3 30.hxg3 e5 31.♕d5+ ♔h8 32.♗xe5 ♕h4 33.♔g2 ♖f8 34.♖e4 ♕g5 35.c7 a5 36.♕d7 ♕c1 37.c8♕

And the game ended in a win for White. The completely paralysed black pieces cannot possibly prevent the advance of the white pawns on the queenside. The blockading position of the queen and bishop on the squares d4 and e5 is instructive. This example would probably have pleased Nimzowitsch.

Conclusion: Not quantity, but quality!

Forces which are ready to take great risks to achieve the aim, are good forces! – Emanuel Lasker

Solution 210

Both sides have numerous weaknesses. But it seems that the

black camp has more! On that basis, we should try to exchange minor pieces. But in which order? In the game Kostenko-S.Guliev (Moscow 2004) Black began with the exchange on e4:

25...♘xe4?! 26.♕xe4 ♗xe3 27.fxe3!

Black had forgotten about this possibility.

27...♖ac8??

Upset at having missed the pawn recapture, Black loses the thread of the game. He should have chosen 27...♖f8! 28.♖ac1 ♖f6 and then ...♖df8 and ...♕b5, completely ceding the c-file, but in return, trying to create a strong build-up on the f-file. And although White keeps the initiative, Black has good chances of creating counterplay. It is dangerous to allow Black to feel so comfortable on the kingside.

28.♖ac1 ♕b5 29.♖f1 ♕b7

Black has still not recovered from the shock of 27.fxe3.

30.♖c6

And White's advantage became obvious.

After the game, Kostenko demonstrated the 'correct' line: 25...♗xe3 26.♖xe3 (26.fxe3?! ♕xd5 27.♘xc5 ♖ac8∓) 26...♘xe4 27.♕xe4 (27.♖xe4 a5) 27...♖ec8 and the chances are roughly equal.

However, after 26.♘xd6 ♕d7 27.♘xe8 ♗d4 28.♖ad1! White still is slightly better.

Conclusion: Benefit can often be obtained from exchanges.

Exchanges lie at the heart of chess. – Mikhail Botvinnik

Solution 211

In the game Abergel-S.Guliev (Moscow 2004) time shortage prevented Black from delving sufficiently deeply into the position. But the position requires precisely this! He calculated the following variation: 47...♘e3 48.♗xe3 (48.♗b3? ♘xd1 49.♗xd1 ♖e8+ 50.♔f5 ♖e1–+) 48...fxe3 49.♘xe3 ♖e8+ 50.♗e6 b3 51.♘d1

analysis diagram

51...♖b8 52.♘b2 (52.♗f5 b2 53.♗b1 ♖e8+!) 52...d1♕ 53.♘xd1 b2 54.♘xb2

♖xb2 55.♔f6 ♖b6 56.h4!? and decided that he had few winning chances here.

Then he went over to the variation **47...♖xd5+ 48.♔xd5 fxg3 49.♔e4** (49.♗c5+? ♔f7! 50.♗xb4 ♘e3+! 51.♘xe3 g2−+) **49...♘f4 50.♔f3 g2**

51.♔f2? g1♕+ 52.♔xg1 ♘e2+, which he liked (there was already no time to calculate 47...♘e1).
However, instead of 51.♔f2? White played
51.h4!
and after the moves
51...♔f7 52.hxg5 hxg5 53.♗e3 ♘d5 54.♔xg2 ♘xe3+ 55.♘xe3 b3 56.♘d1 ♔e6 57.♔f3 ♔e5 58.♔e3 g4 59.♔xd2 ♔d4 60.♘f2 g3 61.♘h3 g2 62.♘g1 ♔c4 63.♔c1
the game ended in a draw.
Analysing the game quietly, we can see that in the variation 47...♘e3 Black has no need to force the play. He obtains a winning position by means of the prophylactic 51...♔g7! (instead of 51...♖b8; see analysis diagram above), e.g. 52.♔f5 ♖b8 53.♘b2 ♖f8+ 54.♔e4 ♖f1 or 52.♘b2 ♖d8 53.♔e4 (53.♗g4 h5 54.♗d1 (54.♗xh5 ♖c8!) 54...♖c8 55.♔d4 (55.♗xb3 ♖b8) 55...♖c2! 56.♘d3 b2!−+) 53...d1♕ 54.♘xd1 ♖xd1 55.♗xb3 ♖h1 56.♗e6 ♖e1+! 57.♔f5

♖e3 and White seems to have no defence.
Thus, in the original position, Black is winning.
But now let us look at the continuation 47...♘e1. Here, possible is 48.gxf4 ♘d3+ (48...gxf4 49.♗e4! f3 50.♗c5+ ♔f7 51.♗xb4 and White has great drawing chances) 49.♔e4 ♘xf4 50.♗b3 ♘xh3 51.♗c5+ ♔g7 52.♗xb4 ♔g6 ♔e3. Undoubtedly, in the final position Black is better, but the win looks doubtful.

Conclusion: Character is the corridor of fate.

One doesn't ask for extras from God. − Sergey Dovlatov

Solution 212

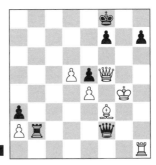

In the game Noruzi-L.Guliev (Lahijan 2005) Black's position looked hopeless, because he was a piece down. However, Black played an interesting rook manoeuvre and won quickly:
41...♖b6! 42.♖h5? ♖g6+ 43.♖g5 ♕g1+ 44.♔h4 ♕h2+
And without waiting for 45.♔g4 h5#, White resigned. In this example, the combined work of rook and queen ended in a beautiful mate.

But whatever one's first impression, the diagram position is in fact equal. White needed to defend accurately. According to the computer, he has two paths to equality:

A) 42.♔h5 ♕e3 (or 42...♖g6 43.♗g4! ♕e3 44.♔h4 h5! 45.♗f3 ♕f2+ 46.♔xh5 ♕e3 47.♔h4 ♕f2+=) 43.♔h4 (43.d6!?) 43...♕f2+ 44.♔h5 ♖g6 45.♗g4 and then as in the variation 42...♖g6;

B) 42.d6 ♖xd6 43.♔h5 ♖g6 (also possible is 43...♕e3) 44.♗g4 ♕d2 45.♔h4 ♕xa2 46.♖h3 ♕b2 47.♖f3 ♕h2+ 48.♖h3 ♕b2=.

Conclusion: A brave deed has two outcomes, victory and defeat.

80% of chess technique consists in coordinating the pieces. – Aron Nimzowitsch

Solution 213

According to Kotov, there are three ways of realising a material advantage: attack, exchange, or transformation into a positional advantage. The correctness of the choice depends on the characteristics of each position. In the game L.Guliev-Saidi (Ahvaz 2005) White exploited his attacking possibilities in a timely fashion:

1.g6! hxg6 2.♗xg6!
The pawn and bishop sacrifice themselves to open a path for the major pieces.
2...♘f6
He also loses after 2...fxg6 3.♕f8+ ♔h7 4.♖f7.
3.♕g3! fxg6
Or 3...♔f8 4.♗xf7! ♔xf7 (4...♕xf7 5.d7) 5.♖xf6+ gxf6 6.♖g1+–.
4.♖xf6 gxf6 5.♕xg6+
And White won.

Conclusion: Victory through attack!

It is a matter of taste whether quietly to follow the beaten track or to seek complications. – Efim Geller

Solution 214

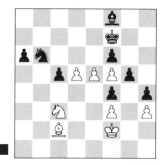

In the game Tunik-S.Guliev (Moscow 2005) White hoped that his pawn minus would be compensated for by the presence of opposite-coloured bishops. In carrying out the break e4-e5, he was counting on opening the game and activating his pieces, exchanging more pawns and also creating a passed pawn, which he could advance. However, without the required piece support, the passed pawn fails to justify White's hopes and soon becomes easy prey for the black pieces. Black has a decisive advantage.

58...c4!

Risky was 58...fxe5 59.♘e4 ♘xd5?? 60.♗b3!.

Now a path is opened for the black bishop, which is ready to support the advance of its pawns (...♗b4) and help to stop the opponent's passed pawn.

59.♘e4

White has no good moves, for example: 59.d6 fxe5 60.♘e4 ♔e8.

59...♘xd5 60.exf6 ♗b4! 61.♗a4 ♘xf6 62.♘xg5+ ♔e7 63.♔e2 ♘d5 64.♘e4 ♘c3+

Sometimes going into an endgame with opposite-coloured bishops is the easiest way to win.

65.♘xc3 ♗xc3 66.♔d1 ♔d6 67.♔c2 ♗f6 0-1

Conclusion: In an endgame with only opposite-coloured bishops, the drawing chances of the weaker side tend to increase, but with additional pieces on the board, by contrast, defending is more difficult, because the bishop often finds itself out of play.

Two people can often save each other where one alone would perish. – Honoré de Balzac

Solution 215

Thanks to Black's scattered forces and offside queen, White is winning. One should especially note the complete readiness of his major pieces to attack.

In the game L.Guliev-Gleizerov (Teheran 2005) White decided the fate of the game by transferring his 'heavy artillery' from the g-file to the h-file:

34.♖g5!! ♕h7 35.♕g4 ♖d2

No help is 35...g6 36.h4! and then h4-h5.

36.♖h5 ♕g6 37.♕h4

An excellent illustration of how to use the major pieces.

37...f6 38.f5!

38.♖h8+? ♔f7 39.♖xa8 e3.

38...exf5

After 38...♕g2 39.♖h8+ ♔f7 40.♕h5+ White mates.

39.e6! ♔f8 40.♖h8+ ♔e7 41.♕f4! ♖d6 42.♖xa8

And after a few more moves, Black resigned.

Conclusion: Sometimes queens and rooks want to imitate the king and move more slowly!

Life is a procession. For someone who is walking at a slow pace, it is too fast, and so he comes out of it. And the one whose

Solution 216

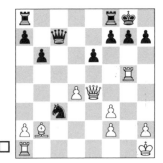

In the game S.Guliev-Grigoriants (Warsaw 2005) White thought for about an hour here, but did not find more than a draw. After the moves **21.♗xc3 ♛xc3 22.♖ag1 g6 23.♖xg6+** the game ended in a handshake, as White gives perpetual check.
The position is equal.

Conclusion: Violent attacks sometimes end in perpetual check.

If aspiration comes from a pure source, then even if it does not succeed completely in reaching the goal, it can be of great benefit. – Ivan Turgenev

Solution 217

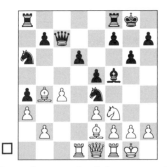

At first glance, Black has a good position. But the excessively

advanced ♘e4 and the weakness of the d6-pawn, as well as the rather cramped position of the ♗f5, make his position hopeless. White is winning.
In the game S.Guliev-Sulskis (Warsaw 2005) the modest move
18.♗d3!
gave White a decisive advantage. The threats include 19.♘h4!, 19.♗xe4 ♗xe4 20.♗xd6, and even 19.g4. There is no defence against all of these simultaneous threats.
18...♘xb4 19.♛xb4 ♛e7
He loses after 19...♖fd8 20.♘h4!, whereas 20.g4 ♘xf2!? looks risky.

20.♗xe4
Again, White does not need to risk the complications of 20.g4 ♘xf2, and instead satisfies himself with a pawn.
20...♗xe4 21.♛xd6
Also good is 21.♖xd6.
21...♖fe8 22.♛xe7 ♖xe7 23.♖d6
And White subsequently realised his extra pawn.

Conclusion: There are the following types of connections: complete (sometimes called 'dead'), incomplete and false.

In chess, according to Smyslov, three things are very important: pins, forks and checks! – Viktor Kupreichik

Solution 218

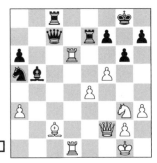

White is winning. In the game Palac-S.Guliev (Warsaw 2005) he quickly demonstrated this:
30.♘h5! ♛xc2
Nothing changes after 30...gxh5 31.f6 followed by 32.♕g3+.
31.♘f6+ ♚g7 32.♕h4 h5 33.♘xh5+ ♚f8 34.♘f6 ♖ec7 35.♕h8+ ♚e7 36.♘g8+ ♖xg8 37.♕f6+
And there is no defence against the threat of 38.♖d8 with mate, so Black resigned.

Conclusion: An unaccompanied king is an easy prey for the enemy forces.

But the emperor is not wearing any clothes! – Hans Christian Andersen

Solution 219

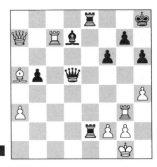

The white pieces are too far away from their king. Therefore, at first glance it seems that after

32...♖e1+! 33.♗xe1 ♖xe1+ 34.♚h2 ♛d1
Black wins. But this appearance is deceptive.
In the game S.Guliev-Lutz (Kusadasi 2006) White played here:
35.♖xg7!
After this counterattack, Black, by means of
35...♖h1+ 36.♚g3 ♛d6+ 37.♚f3 ♛d5+ 38.♚g3 ♛d6+ 39.♚f3 ♛d5+ 40.♚g3 ♛d6+
gave perpetual check.
As shown by the following variations, 36...♛d3+? 37.♕e3 or 37.f4? ♛d3+ 38.♚f2 ♖f1#, neither side can avoid the draw.

Conclusion: An exchange of blows often cancels out.

Confucius was once asked: 'How should one answer kindness?' He replied 'With kindness.' And to the question how should one react to evil, he replied 'Fairly!'

Solution 220

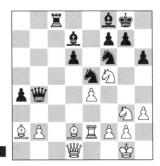

In the game Soltanici-S.Guliev (Kusadasi 2006) White had just played 27.♗f4-d2 in full confidence that the b2-pawn was untouchable. With a close look at the position, you will probably see that the pawn

can be taken, and this move leads to an advantage for Black. There followed

27...♕xb2 28.♗xh6 ♕a3 29.♗g5 ♘h7! 30.♗e3

(30.♗f4 ♘d3!)

30...♗b5! 31.♖c2 ♖xc2 32.♕xc2 ♗d3 33.♕d2 ♘c4 34.♗xc4 ♗xc4 35.♗d4 ♕d3!

and Black obtained a large advantage. Soon the pressure from his pieces became irresistible.

Conclusion: By which system do you develop your technique of calculating variations?

Calculation of variations, according to Kotov, is one of the foundations on which chess creativity is based. – Viktor Golenishchev

People are divided into the reasoning and the creative. – Nikolaj Roerich

Solution 221

At first glance, White needs to resign. However, he has at his disposal a tactical operation, which completely changes this hasty assessment. White is winning!

1.♖xh7+! ♔xh7 2.♕h3+ ♔g8

Or 2...♔g7 3.♕h6+ ♔g8 4.♘f6+ ♕xf6 5.exf6 ♖a7 6.♗e7; 2...♕h5 3.♘f6+.

3.♘f6+ ♕xf6 4.♕xc8+

This forcing variation could have decided the game in White's favour. However, in the game S.Guliev-Alexandrov (Sharjah 2007) White missed this combination and lost.

Conclusion: Don't miss your chances!

There is no fog from which there is no exit. The main thing is to hang on and keep moving forward. – Romain Rolland

Solution 222

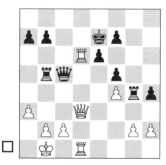

In this position, thanks to his complete control of the d-file, White is winning. At first glance the black king is safe and, in an extreme case, it can flee to the kingside. However, White has an excellent combinative solution:

1.c4! ♖b6 2.♖c6!!+− ♖xb2+

Or 2...♖xc6 (2...♕xc6) 3.♕d8#.

3.♔xb2 ♖xg2+ 4.♔a1 ♕a5 5.♖c5

And in the game L.Guliev-Kotanjian (Moscow 2007) Black resigned.

Conclusion: In chess, as in life, sometimes one member of a team sacrifices himself to open a path for another, stronger member.

Talent is a spark of God, which man usually burns himself, illuminating the path of others with this own fire. – Vasily Kluchevsky

Solution 223

Black is better. It seems that because of the loss of the d6-pawn, he faces a difficult time, but thanks to the following typical manoeuvre, it turns out that the chances are on his side. In the game Scherbakov-L. Guliev (Moscow 2007) Black played:
1...♗f8!!
The threat of 2...♗h6 compels White to go in for a forcing variation:
2.♘xd6+ ♖xd6 3.♖xd6 ♗xd6 4.♖xd6 f5 5.gxf5 exf5 6.♔d2?
Black's position is also clearly preferable after 6.♖d4!? ♖g8! (6...♖h4? 7.♔d2 ♖xf4 8.♔e3 ♖h4 9.exf5±) 7.♔d1 ♖g2 8.♖d2 ♖g1+ 9.♔e2 fxe4 10.♔f2 ♖b1 11.♖e2 f5 (11...♖xb2? 12.c3!) 12.b3 ♔e7 13.♗h5 ♔d6.
6...fxe4 7.♗e2 ♔e7 8.♖d4 ♖g8 9.♔e3 ♖g2 10.♖d1 ♖xh2 11.♖e1 ♖g2 12.♖h1 h2 13.c4 a5 14.b3 ♔f6 15.c5 ♔f5 16.♗f1 ♖g3+ 17.♔f2 ♔xf4 18.♖xh2 e3+ 19.♔e1 ♖g1
And Black won.

Conclusion: Using knowledge in practice requires a creative approach.

Knowledge is a weapon, not an aim. – Alexey Tolstoy

Solution 224

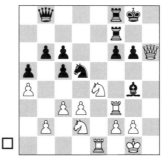

The game L.Guliev-Lazarev (Albacete 2007) ended in a draw after the moves:
1.♖g3 ♗f5 2.♘c4 ♖h7 3.♕d2 ♔h8 4.d4 cxd4 5.cxd4
However, this should not mislead you. White has a large advantage, one almost wants to say a decisive one. He just needs to be courageous and sacrifice the queen.
The correct continuation was as follows: **1.♕xg6+! ♖g7 2.♘xf6+ ♘xf6 3.♖xf6 ♖xg6 4.♖xg6+ ♔h7** (nothing is changed by 4...♔f7) **5.♖xg4** and Black can hardly hope to survive.

Conclusion: An advantage acquired over dozens of moves can be lost in just one.

Life is like a mountain – one climbs slowly, but falls quickly. – Guy de Maupassant

Index of players (numbers refer to pages)

Bibliography

Books mentioned in the text:
José Raul Capablanca, *Chess Fundamentals*, Gloucester Publishers Pic, ed. 1994
Max Euwe, *The Middle Game*, Ishi Press 2012
Robert Greene, *The 48 Laws of Power*, Penguin Books 2000
Vlastimil Hort, Vlastimil Jansa, *The Best Move*, RHM Press 1980
Alexander Kotov, *Think Like a Grandmaster*, Anova 2002
Aron Nimzowitsch, *My System & Chess Praxis*, New In Chess 2016
Alexander Panchenko, *Theory and Practice of Chess Endings*, vol. 1 and 2, Convekta LTD 2009
Francois-André Danican Philidor, *Analysis of the Game of Chess*, P. Elmsly 1790

Periodicals:
Chess Informant
New In Chess
Shakhmaty v SSSR

Engines used:
Houdini 6
Komodo 10
Stockfish 9

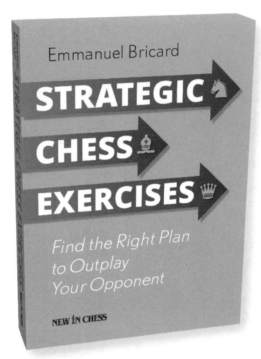